LEARNING
LEVEL II

by
David A. Lien

COMPUSOFT PUBLISHING
A Division of CompuSoft, Inc.
P.O. Box 19669 • San Diego, California 92119 U.S.A.

A Personal Note From The Author

Greetings again from the land of fruit and nuts!

It's been awhile since we've shared the fun of learning to use our TRS-80 Computer at Level I. Hearing from so many of you who took the time to write kind notes about the Level I book, and meeting so many readers from around the world who said "I learned about computers from you" has been a source of great personal satisfaction. We've done our best to repeat the act at Level II.

Learning Level II is written in the same style you wanted continued — with the emphasis on LEARNING. So, like your Level I User's/ Learner's Manual, it is designed to teach — and your computer is the laboratory. This manual, along with your imagination, is all you need.

So sit back again, relax, and savor it. Whether you're upgrading from Level I to Level II or starting out with a brand new Level II machine, a relaxed but confident approach is important. I'll furnish the rest. Every word of the "Personal Note" on page 1 of your Level I Manual applies here, too!

Enjoy your new (or upgraded) Computer.

Dr. David A. Lien
San Diego — 1979

Acknowledgements

Because so many asked for this book, they must be the first acknowledged. *You* asked for it — *you* got it! I sincerely hope it meets your expectations.

To the Baileys of Iowa and California go special thanks for supplying quiet hideaways. Without the long, uninterrupted sessions at the Ranch, in Rural Iowa and the Beach, this book never would have been completed.

Dave Waterman roughed out the section on interpreting error messages and the Chapters on using the Interface and Dual Cassettes.

CompuSoft secretary Nancy Burns, having never used a computer, made the ideal "guinea pig" and wrang out the upgraded Level I Manual on a Level II machine.

Having been in the author's head for two years made *Learning Level II* harder to finally bring to paper — not easier. Dave Gunzel, the master Editor, pulled it all together into this attractive, coherent package.

Last but not least, Leway Composing Service of Fort Worth, Texas designed the book and set the type. Their high quality work on our *The BASIC Handbook* has prompted many favorable comments from those in-the-know.

Cartoons by Rich Barnes

Table of Contents
For
LEARNING LEVEL II
(A Ribald Novel in 3 Parts . . .)

APPENDIX

PART I

Upgrading the LEVEL I Manual

Updating The

Level I User's Manual

Remember the good old days, scribbling with a stubby crayon, cutting out paper and getting glue in our hair?

WE GET TO DO IT AGAIN!

A little of this "sandbox" work on the side, and we'll quickly work our way through Elementary BASIC and then move on to the Intermediate BASIC of *Learning Level II* (that's Part II and III of this neat book).

As a quick flip through Part I shows, most changes to the *Level I User's Manual* are simple "mark-ups" with a pen. A few pages require such extensive changing however that replacement pages are provided ... **twice!** Once, in Part I. Again, in Appendix Z where you cut them out and paste or tape them over the obsolete sections in the Level I Manual. (We printed them twice so you won't have to cut up the main part of this book.)

So, grab a pen and the *Level I User's Manual*, turn to the next page, and away we go ...

START HERE!

The BASICs Are Everything

We have taken some unique and innovative approaches in this book because so many of you are upgrading from Level I and so are already competent at Introductory BASIC. However, some of you are starting fresh with a Level II machine — you got a Learner's Manual written for Level I, and a Level II Reference book — and that won't do at all! Level II was only a gleam in the eye when the Level I book was written. Not worry however. We can fix-um.

In nearly every field of endeavor, the BASICs are all-important. What good are books to a non-reader? What good is algebra to someone who can't even add? If a foundation is faulty, it doesn't matter what is built above it.

These pearls of wisdom are directed especially to those of you who own a Level II machine and have not gone thru the Level I Manual. It is important that you take advantage of the extensive work done by the author in updating the Level I Manual to make that Manual work with your new Level II Computer (that's what Part I is all about). To fail to do so would defeat your own desire to become as powerful as your Computer.

Part I of this book is dedicated entirely to new TRS-80 owners. If you're one of these, YOU **must** begin your foray into the not-so-difficult computer field with Part I and the Level I User's Manual which came with the Computer. Enter the updating changes from Part I into the Level I Manual as you go, a chapter at a time. When you have mastered the Level I Manual, continue on to Part II of this book. It's all very simple once you get rolling.

"Old Timers" who cut their teeth on Level I BASIC need only spend an hour or so reviewing Part I and updating their old Level I Manual for future reference. You can then proceed directly to Part II of *Learning Level II* and be on your way to yet greater glory and, er oblivion.

Changes in pages 1 - 6

☑ Page 5, right column, item 3B: If you have a CTR-80 Recorder, cross out all references to the dummy plug.

(Use the check box to check off ☑ as you make the change)

Level II BASIC requires a different Volume control setting for the Tape Recorder.

☑ Page 5, 8 lines from the bottom, change the words highlighted in heavy type

> have the CRT-41's Volume control set between **3 and 5.** Then press the

☑ On page 6, right column, line 4 change to read:

> board should light up and the screen should show
> MEMORY SIZE?_

Press the ENTER **key once and it will display**

RADIO SHACK LEVEL II BASIC

READY

>

Changes in Chapter 1

Level I BASIC had a nice feature called "Radio Shack Shorthand" which, unfortunately, went the way of all good things (like that first car. Mine was a 1931 Chevrolet Cabriolet. Sold it for $50 to get college money. Saw one the other day for $5,000. Aaaaaagh!!!!).

The "Shorthand" was very handy, but Level II replaced it with other, more powerful features. The Level I Manual uses "shorthand" frequently, so we'll have to go through and change those places to "longhand". Take a quick glance at the Level I Manual's inside back cover for a listing of the entire "LEVEL I Shorthand Dialect". Don't bother studying it tho (too late now!).

☑ Page 7, Center of page, step 3 needs to be changed to:

MEMORY SIZE?_ will appear. Press **ENTER** and get a display

RADIO SHACK LEVEL II BASIC

READY

>_

The first place "shorthand" appears is on page 7, near the bottom. Change P.M. to PRINT MEM in both places. (Go ahead — do it! Grab a pen and start making the changes. If you ruin the manual you can always get another one at the Radio Shack store. Cat. No. 26-2101.)

In addition, in the third "shaded" comment area in the far right-hand comments column, scratch out the entire first line.

Change the fourth comment in the "shaded" area to read:

If you have 4K of memory, the number should be 3284. With 8K of memory, it should be 738∅. With 16K it should be 15572.

Also, at the bottom of page 7, the number which will appear after PRINT MEM is **15572** instead of 3583 (make the same changes in the first paragraph on page 8).

☐ On page 9, cross out the third shaded area.

Changes in Chapter 2

Here is our first "cut and paste" job. This and all other "cut-outs" are duplicated at the back of the book so you won't have to mutilate this main part.

Grab scissors and cut out the replacement (from the back of the book) for the bottom part of page 11. Tape or glue it over the existing text.

Oh — sorry about that! It "bombed", didn't it? The screen said

    ?SN ERROR

We deliberately "set you up" to demonstrate the Computer's ERROR troubleshooter. The Computer is smart enough to know when you've made a mistake in telling it what to do, and so it prints a clue as to the nature of the error. In this case, the ? tells you that it doesn't understand what you are saying. The SN stands for the word "syntax" (an obscure word that refers to the pattern of words in a language). ERROR means you have made one. Later on we'll learn how to make the Computer accept a "YES" or "NO" and respond accordingly.

There are dozens of possible errors we can make, and in good time we will learn the 23 "ERROR CODES" built into Level II. Meanwhile, there is just one other important ERROR situation which you should be able to recognize so you can pry yourself out of accidental trouble. Let's retype line 20 and deliberately make a spelling error:

    20 PRIMT "YOU CALLED, MASTER. DO YOU
                  HAVE A COMMAND?"

and   RUN   **ENTER**

(All the type should be on one line, but we can't fit it on the page in this book. We'll do that quite often, so better get used to it.)

Again we get an ERROR message

    ?SN ERROR IN 20

but after READY instead of a prompt we get

    20_

This tells us that the error is in line 2∅, and by pressing the **ENTER** key, line 2∅ will be printed in full so we can look for the error and correct it. (Shhh! If you know what else it will let us do don't say anything yet. We don't want to confuse anyone with too much too soon.)

Retype line 2∅ to correct the misspelling in PRIMT before continuing on.

☑ Page 13, change line 21 to read:

accepts Line numbers up to **65529.**

☑ Page 14, change line 7 to read:

65529. This requires two steps.

☑ Page 14, change last program line to:

65529   END   **ENTER**

☐ Page 14, change 3rd line from the bottom to:

Move END from **#65529** to line #17, then RUN . . .

☑ Page 15, delete the first 2 paragraphs. Also, delete the words WHAT? and HOW? from under Miscellaneous, plus the entire shaded area at the right.

Changes in Chapter 3

☑ Page 17, change the last line to:

simple READY

>

☑ Page 20, change the 9th line up from the bottom to:

puter divides up the screen width into four zones of **16** characters each. When a PRINT

Changes in Chapter 4

NONE

Changes in Chapter 5

NONE

Changes in Chapter 6

NONE

Changes in Chapter 7

NONE

Changes in Chapter 8

☑ Page 37, change the last line to:

1

☑ Page 38, delete entire first paragraph.

☑ Page 38, change lines 17 and 18 to read:

> grams. If you turn the Computer off, **then on again, all variables will be set to Ø. Typing RUN also "initializes" the variables to Ø.**

☑ Page 39, in the first 4 lines, change all 3583's to 15572 and 4Ø96 to 16384

In the top shaded area, the last 4 lines should read:

> once more. (If your TRS-80 has **less** RAM, you can expect a **smaller** number, as follows:
>
> 8K RAM: 738Ø
> 4K RAM: 3284.)

☑ Page 39, replace the rest of page with the following, starting with line 11. (Again, clip from the back of the book.)

15561

The program you entered took $15572 - 15561 = 11$ bytes of space. Here is how you can account for it:

1. Each line number and the space following it (regardless of how small or large that line number is) occupies 4 memory cells. The "carriage return" at the end of the line takes 1 more byte, even though it does not print on the screen. Thus, memory "overhead" for each line, short or long is 5 bytes.

2. Each letter, number and space takes 1 byte. In the above program 5 bytes for overhead + 6 bytes for the characters = 11 bytes.

Now, type RUN, then check the memory again with PRINT MEM . It changed to 15554 — 7 more bytes! When RUN, a simple variable like the A takes up 3 bytes and the numerical value takes another 4 — totaling 7.

We will be studying memory requirements in more detail in *Learning Level II,* but this gives you a brief introduction.

☑ Page 40, delete first 2 lines

☑ Page 40, delete lines 7 thru 12

☑ Page 40, delete SORRY from the last line

☐ Page 40, delete the shaded comment area.

Changes in Chapter 9

☑ Page 41, line 9 should read:

tape, or loaded from tape, in **under** 3 minutes. Most programs are shorter and take even less

☑ Page 41, 4 lines up from the bottom. Change CASVE to

CSAVE . "A"

☑ Page 41, if you are using a CTR-80, delete the third shaded area down from the top.

☑ Page 41, the bottom shaded area should continue:

"A" is our name for the program. Every program must have a "name" consisting of one letter or number enclosed in quotes.

☐ Page 42, number 7. If you have a CTR-80 recorder, you'll notice that the REM jack is not labeled (it's the one holding the smallest plug). Doesn't matter in any case since the REWIND key works on this special recorder **without** pulling the REM plug. So if you use a CTR-80, cross out the words:

Disconnect the small plug from the recorder's REM jack and

☑ Page 42, change number 2 to:

Push down the PLAY button until it locks. Set the Volume control to about **5**.

☐ Page 42, change line 9 under **Loading** to:

puter's memory at the rate of about **2400** bytes per minute.

☑ Page 42, change the 5th line up from the bottom to:

Volume is set to **5** . . .

Changes in Chapter 10

☑ Page 45, be sure that RUN is in the last line.

☑ Page 46, change line 19 to:

FOR-NEXT loops can be stepped by any **decimal** number, even negative numbers. Why one

☑ Page 46, change the 4th line up from the bottom to read:

from 1 to 5. Line 1Ø still got printed 5 times. **Change the STEP from −1 to −2.5 and RUN again. Amazing!**

☑ Page 48, change the 4th line up from the bottom to read:

vious program. **(With Level II, typing RUN automatically resets all the variables back to Ø before the program executes.)**

Changes in Chapter 11

☑ Page 53, under "Solutions For Sale", cross out all of #1 and replace with the following:

Pressing a SHIFT key and the @ key *at the same time* **will stop program execution or a LISTing. Pressing almost any key will start it running again. RUN the program a number of times, practicing stopping and starting it using "shift-at".**

☑ Page 53, delete the top shaded comments block.

☑ Page 53, lower shaded block, cross out these words:

but it's not a very useful one
That's even messier than the first one.

☐ Page 54. Add a note in the right column:

When listing a program that has more than 16 lines and the lines you want to see scroll off the top of the screen, you can use the `BREAK` **key to stop the LISTing where you want it.**

Make these changes in Level I User's Manual

21

☑ Page 54, change program line 2 (in The Egg Timer) to:

    2 FOR X = 1 TO 37ØØ

☐ Page 54, change the 2nd line in paragraph below the program to:

    can do approximately **37Ø** FOR-NEXT loops per second. That means, by specifying the

☑ Page 54, the Answer should be:

    2 FOR X = 1 TO 111ØØ

☐ Page 183 contains the answer to Exercise 11-1. Change program line 3 to read:

    3 P = 37Ø

☑ Page 55, delete both shaded areas, and replace the page with the following:

How to Handle Long Program Listings

We now have two programs in the Computer. Let's pull a LIST to look at them. My, my — they are so long it won't all fit on the screen. Now what do we do?

Rather than wring our hands about the problem, type each of the following variations of LIST, and watch the screen very carefully as each does its thing:

    LIST 5Ø (Lists only line 5Ø)

    LIST −5Ø (Lists all lines up thru 5Ø)

    LIST 5Ø− (Lists all lines from 5Ø to end)

LIST 3Ø-7Ø (Lists all lines from 3Ø thru 7Ø)

LIST 4-85 (Note that these numbers are not even in
the program)

How's that for something to write home about?

Questions: How would you look at the resident program up through line 9? *ANSWER:* type LIST −9 (Talk about a give away!)

☑Page 56, in the shaded area, delete "Again," and add this note in the right hand column:

Try starting the program(s) at different numbers. As you do, different (but very predictable) results occur. Don't worry about the strange error messages. We'll be studying them in great detail in *Learning Level II,* **where we have a real need for them.**

☑Page 56, change lines 4 and 5 under **Meanwhile, Back At the Ranch** to read:

our big program. First, let's erase the test program **by typ-**ing DELETE 1-9 **ENTER** Then type LIST to see what happened. Wow! How's that for power?

The variations of DELETE **somewhat resemble** LIST###**, but only** DELETE### **,**DELETE-###**, and** DELETE ###-### **will work.**

☑Page 57, add this note at the top right.

CONT stands for CONTINUE

☑Page 59, change item #2 to:

Total circuit power (circuit current squared, times **circuit resistance)** $I^2 * (1Ø + R)$

☑ Page 188, delete the shaded comment.

☑ Page 6Ø, under **Commands** add DELETE###. Under **Miscellaneous** delete ⬆ Up-Arrow.

Changes in Chapter 12

☑ Page 61, program line 1Ø, remove the space between TAB and (5)

☑ Page 62, change line 3 to:

Whether you follow TAB(##) with a semicolon or not makes no difference. In either

☑ Page 62, add the following note in the right column:

A semicolon is traditionally used following TAB, as shown. Some interpreters allow a comma instead (as in Level I). Level II and most later BASIC interpreters allow a blank or even nothing at all.

Experiment to see which you like best.

☑ Page 63, computer program line 2ØØ, the first TAB should contain the number **5**, not 5Ø.

☑ Page 63, program line 21Ø, remove space between TAB and (2Ø).

Changes in Chapter 13

☑ Page 67, change lines 2 and 3 to:

counting A's and B's as they whiz by, you remember what to do. Just press the **Shift and** @ **keys at the same time** to stop execution and temporarily freeze the display. The **BREAK** key and typing

☑ Page 67, replace lines 13 and 14 with:

```
?NF ERROR IN 6Ø
```

Changes in Chapter 14

☑ Page 7Ø, change the last program line to:

```
Z = .14159
```

☑ Page 7Ø, delete last 3 lines.

☑ Page 71, delete first paragraph.

☑ Page 71, first line of second paragraph, delete LEVEL I BASIC

☑ Page 71, 2nd to last paragraph, change last line as follows:

X into an integer and fractional part. **It's on page 7Ø.**

☑ Page 71, change last paragraph to:

We clearly **can** just go on taking the INT value of X over and over to try and split **out the digits.** Let's try it with Z.

☑ Page 72, lines 4, 9, and 19, .141589 should be **.14159**

☑ Page 73, change line 2 to:

```
95 FOR A = 1 TO 5
```

☑ Page 73, line 17. Cross out L = 9.

☑ Page 73, replace all the explanation under the "print-out" with the following:

They are all there, but what gives with the last value of L. L = 8 ??? it's supposed to be 9!

Well, let's analyze the program first, then worry about that little detail.

Line 95 began a FOR-NEXT loop with 5 passes, one for each of the 5 digits right of the decimal.

Line 12Ø creates a new decimal value of M (just a temporary storage location) by stripping off the integer part. (Plugging in the values, M = 1.4159 − 1 = X .4159)

Line 13Ø does the same as line 9Ø did, multiplying the new decimal value times 1Ø so as to make the left-hand digit an integer and vulnerable to being snatched away by the INT function. (M = .4159 * 1Ø = 4.159)

Line 14Ø moves the control back to line 95 for another pass through the clipping program . . . and the rest is history.

Now about that little detail . . . the wrong value of the last digit. As you have noticed in this lesson, we have repeatedly scratched out the 8 from the number .141589 — a real problem in Level I. We just about escaped the problem in Level II, but not quite.

Back in Chapter 8 we talked about the problem of computer error when getting into the land of little numbers. We've now plowed head-on into that problem. To understand it better, change line 95 to read:

```
95 FOR A = 1 TO 1Ø
```

and RUN .

Where did all those other numbers come from? (Beats me.) Again, as we told you in Chapter 8, the last digit or 2 at the end of a number is not to be trusted as being high-precision.

But there is a solution. Change line 95 back as it was, then change line 3Ø to read:

```
3Ø X = 3.141590Ø
```

and RUN

Whew! Had us a little nervous there for a while . . . but then success. By our declaring that the accuracy of X is to be a few decimal places greater than we really need, we then are assured that those digits we do need are reliable. There are other ways to do this and we will learn them in *Learning Level II*.

But let's not get diverted from the main theme of this Chapter.

☑ Page 75, change line 1 to:

There it is. All the data you can handle (and then some). By using the **SHIFT and @ keys**

Changes in Chapter 15

☑Page 77, in the shaded area, change line 7 to:

up to **256** characters (including line number and

☑Page 77, in the shaded area, change line 9 to:

up **four** Display lines; but it's still just one program

☑Page 8Ø, Delete lines 4, 5, and 6; also, change line 7 to:

It is possible to create or simulate func-

☑Page 83, add this Exercise 15-2:

Remove all traces of the subroutine from the resident program. Use the SGN function that is already built into Level II to accomplish the same thing we have been doing using a subroutine. Hint: T = SGN(X)

Changes in Chapter 16

☑Page 87, replace lines 6 and 7 with

1 2 3 4 5

?OD ERROR IN 3Ø   (**OD means Out of Data**)

☑Page 88, add the following note at the side:

In LEVEL II BASIC we can use all 26 letters of the alphabet for string variables, just like with plain old numeric variables. It gets even better when you master this manual and get back into the full-blown *Learning Level II.*

☑ Page 88, change line 13 to:

and/or Combinations of letters, numbers and spaces. Type NEW

☑ Page 88, watch the spacing on program line 3Ø. It should be:

```
3Ø PRINT "SEE MY FOXY ";A$
```

☑ Page 89, delete lines 2 and 3. Changes lines 4 and 5 to read:

Let's use 2 string variables to **accomplish the same thing, seeing how they work with each other. Rework the program to read**

☑ Page 89, Program line 3Ø should have a space between the Y in FOXY and the quote. Delete EXERCISE 16-1 and the rest of the page, including the second shaded comment.

☑ Page 9Ø, delete entire page.

☑ Page 91, delete entire page.

☐ Page 92, Under Miscellaneous, delete (Y/N)-Teaching etc.

Changes in Chapter 17

NONE

Changes in Chapter 18

☑ Page 95, delete entire page.

☑ Page 96, delete lines 8 thru 15.

☑ Page 96, lines 17 and 18 should read:

> Control yourself! It's easy to get carried away. While we will be using multiple statement lines often from here on, you will quickly see that it's

☑ Page 96, 2nd to last paragraph, delete first two lines and change the third line to:

> Multiple statement lines require careful understanding.

☑ Page 96, in the shaded area, delete the last 3 lines.

☑ Page 97, note that the program incorporates some Level I Shorthand. Eliminating the shorthand, here is how it should read:

```
1Ø INPUT "TYPE IN A NUMBER";X

2Ø IF X = 3 THEN 5Ø : GOTO 7Ø

3Ø PRINT "HOW DID YOU GET HERE?"

4Ø END

5Ø PRINT "X=3"

6Ø END

7Ø PRINT "CAN'T GET FROM THERE TO HERE."
```

From this, you should be able to understand the rest of the page. Change EXERCISE 18-1 to read:

Using the Shorthand you have picked up incidentally so far and that found on the back inside cover, convert the one on page 214 titled *Loan Amortization* **into Level II BASIC. We have learned everything found in that program, so with a bit of effort and clear thinking you should be able to do the job. The experience will come in handy when converting other programs from various sources written in Level I BASIC, as well as understanding the remainder of this Level I book.**

☑Page 98, under **Miscellaneous**, delete LEVEL I shorthand dialect

Changes in Chapter 19

☑Page 1ØØ, 4th line up from the bottom, change to:

3. The largest permissible value of X is 32767.

☑Page 1Ø1. Here's a good chance for you to practice a little translating from Level I shorthand to Level II BASIC. Write in the right hand column:

P. = PRINT. IN. = INPUT. F. = FOR. G. = GOTO.

N. = NEXT.

☑Page 1Ø4: Replace program lines 1 and 2 with

```
1 RANDOM
```

Changes in Chapter 20

☑Page 1∅8, delete lines 12, 13, and 14.

☑Page 111, change the shaded block to:

Of course you haven't forgotten how to do that have you!
Type ERASE . . . no, no, no! Type NEW.

☑Page 112, change the program to read:

```
16 IF V+A<48 GOTO 2∅

18 PRINT "TOO MANY VERTICAL BLOCKS.
                    NOT ENOUGH ROOM!"
```

☑Page 112, add a shaded area.
Remember, you can't draw pictures off the screen. If you get an error message like ?FC ERROR IN 7∅, that means you tried to do it.

☑Page 115, add a shaded area with the same message as above.

☑Page 115, change the first line to:

```
1∅ INPUT "VERTICAL ADDRESS (1 TO 47)";Y
```

☑Page 115, in the middle program, add this program line:

```
11 REM Y MUST BE LARGER THAN ∅
```

☑Page 115, sixth line up from the bottom, change to:

down.

☑Page 115, last program, change line 2∅ to:

```
2∅ INPUT "VERTICAL STARTING POINT
                  (1 TO 47)";Y
```

☑ Page 116, the program at the top of the page, add a line 65:

```
65 IF Y = 48 GOTO 99
```

☑ Page 116, delete lines 12 through 14 and the shaded area.

☑ Page 116, program lines 1Ø and 4Ø, change to:

```
1Ø INPUT "HORIZONTAL STARTING POINT
                (1 TO 127)";Y

4Ø RESET(X-1,Y)
```

☑ Page 116, add a new line 65 in the bottom program:

```
65 IF X=128 GOTO 99
```

☑ Page 117, delete top 9 lines.

☑ Page 117, change the following program lines:

```
2Ø INPUT "VERTICAL STARTING POINT
                (1 TO 2Ø)";Y

3Ø INPUT "LOWER BARRIER (3Ø TO 47)";K

8Ø RESET(X,Y-1)
```

☑ Page 118, delete program lines 11Ø and 12Ø

☑ Page 118, change first program line 13Ø to:

```
13Ø IF Y<K THEN 8Ø
```

☑ Page 118, change program line 8Ø to:

```
8Ø RESET(64,Y-D)
```

Changes in Chapter 21

☑ Page 124, top shaded area, change line 5 to:

```
A$ = "(YOUR NAME)"
```

☑ Page 125, change line 15 to:

Remember, its name is "A". Its elements are numbered.

☑ Page 126, delete last line on the page

☑ Page 127, add this at the top of the right column:

Awwk!! What is this ?BS business? Well, since arrays take up a lot of memory space, the TRS-80 automatically allows us to use up to only 11 array elements without question. (They can be numbered from 0 to 10.) Then our credit runs out. We earlier used elements numbered from 1 to 10 without any problem.

To use array elements numbered beyond 10 in the array called "A", we have to "reDEMension" the array space available. Our highest number in Array "A" needs to be 110, so we'll add a program line:

```
5 DIM A(210)
```

and RUN again

☑ Page 127, delete the first 10 lines.

☑ Page 127, change line 11 to:

Let's just arbitrarily assign array locations 101 through 110 to

☑ Page 127, delete all 3 shaded areas.

☑ Top of page 196, add:

```
5 DIM A(21Ø)
```

☑ Page 129, change program line 3Ø to:

```
DIM A(52) : FOR C=1 TO 52 : READ A(C) : NEXT C
```

☑ Page 131, delete last 9 lines.

☑ Page 132, delete first 8 lines and the shaded area

Changes in Chapter 22

☑ Page 133, add this note to the top right margin:

> **Level II BASIC uses the character @ in place of the word AT, so every reference to AT should be changed to @. PRINT AT and P.AT should always be replaced with PRINT@. (EXTREME CAUTION: DO NOT USE THE SHIFT KEY WITH @.) Make these changes as you go along in this Chapter, and in the User Programs in Part C as you use them.**

☑ Page 133, these are the type changes to make throughout this Chapter.

Line 11, change to:

Learn something new every day. The PRINT@ state-

Line 14, change to:

```
5Ø PRINT@2ØØ,"HELLO THERE 2ØØ, WHEREVER YOU ARE."
```

☑Page 134, make these program line changes:

```
2Ø PRINT@4Ø7, "H    M    S"

6Ø      PRINT@47Ø,H,":"M;M;":";S

7Ø      FOR N = 1 TO 31Ø : NEXT N

11Ø GOTO 1Ø
```

☑Page 134, 2nd line up from the bottom, change to:

the TRS-80 with LEVEL **II** BASIC will execute somewhere around **3ØØ** simple FOR-NEXT

☑Page 135, 2nd line, change to:

timepiece (increasing or decreasing the "**3ØØ**" figure as
needed). Over the short run, this is

☑Page 135, change program line 8Ø to read:

```
8Ø RESET (64,Y-D)
```

☑Page 136-137, replace the Graph Display program with this
one:

```
1Ø CLS

2Ø PRINT@2Ø, "G R A P H   H E A D I N G"

3Ø PRINT@84,"- - - -   - - - - - - -"

4Ø REM * HORIZONTAL MARKERS *

5Ø FOR X = 1 TO 59

6Ø PRINT@9ØØ+X,".";

7Ø NEXT X
```

```
8Ø REM * HORIZONTAL NUMBERS *

9Ø FOR X = Ø TO 5

1ØØ PRINT@964+1Ø*X,X;

11Ø NEXT X

12Ø REM * VERTICAL MARKERS *

13Ø FOR Y = Ø TO 13

14Ø PRINT@Y*64+68,"-"

15Ø NEXT Y

16Ø REM * VERTICAL NUMBERS *

17Ø FOR Y = Ø TO 13

18Ø PRINT@Y*64+64,13-Y;

19Ø NEXT Y

999 GOTO 999
```

☑ Page 137, the second line of the first shaded area, change to:

form . . . true or yes = −1 and false or no gives a Ø.

☑ Page 137, fourth line under "What is the POINT of all this?", change to:

with the address of X, Y. If that point is lit, the POINT statement says "−1". If it is dark, the

☑ Page 137, third line up from the bottom, change to:

Since we had not lit 3Ø,3Ø the answer came back with Ø.

☑Page 137, delete the last 2 lines on the page and the second shaded area.

☑Page 138, change the Let There Be Light program to:

```
1Ø X=75 : Y=2Ø

2Ø INPUT "DO YOU WISH TO LIGHT THE BLOCK
                    (1 = YES Ø = NO)";Q

3Ø CLS

4Ø IF Q = Ø GOTO 8Ø

5Ø SET(X,Y)

6Ø GOTO 1ØØ

8Ø RESET(X,Y)

1ØØ IF POINT(X,Y) = -1 PRINT@2ØØ,X;Y
                            "IS LIT"

2ØØ IF POINT(X,Y) = Ø PRINT@2ØØ,X;Y,
                            "IS DARK"

999 GOTO 999
```

☑Page 138, 6 lines up from the bottom, change to:

that occur. This 2 minute "moving picture" really tells all you need to know about the

☐Page 138-139, delete program line 19Ø and put PRINT@ in its proper form; also eliminate the Level I shorthand.

☑Page 14Ø, delete lines 11, 12, and 13.

Changes in Chapter 23

No Changes

Changes in Chapter 24

☑ Page 148, replace program line 1∅ with:

```
1∅ CLS:PRINT"TYPE A '1' FOR YES,
                AND A '∅' FOR NO"
```

☑ Page 148, change line 17 to:

Line 1∅ clears the screen and gives operating instructions.

☑ Page 149, add the following in the right column:

First the BAD news.

The + and * as used in the rest of the programs works fine in Level I BASIC, however the logic doesn't always act logical when the going gets rough.

But, the GOOD news is that Level II BASIC let's us use the actual words AND and OR instead of the Mathematical symbols, and they work just fine!

Here then is our opportunity to get some drill in converting + and * to OR and AND. Wherever there is "mixed logic", using both * and + in the same program line, (as in the Teachers Pet, next) switch over to the words AND and OR. * and + can be used as shown in the easier ones which follow. You should be able to switch back and forth between the words and symbols interchangeably.

☑ Page 15∅, change line 18 to:

out the surprise caused by the logical **AND** in line 4∅. Type this program in, and RUN.

☑Page 152, change the program lines to read as follows:

```
2Ø PRINT"ANSWER WITH A 1 FOR YES &
                         Ø FOR NO"

3Ø PRINT

1ØØ IF (A=Ø)+(B=Ø)+(C=Ø)+(D=Ø)+(E=Ø)
                         THEN 13Ø
```

☑Page 153, add the following at the top of the right column:

An additional benefit of the changes in Level II handling of AND and OR is that the parenthesis found at Level I can be omitted (at least in straightforward uses). Go back and enter a program or two omitting the parenthesis and using the logical words, just to get a feel for how it looks.

☐Page 199, cross out the last line.

Changes in Chapter 25

☐ Chapter 25 can be deleted. Level II has added a number of so-called "Library" Functions which make the use of many advanced subroutines unecessary. The use of Square Roots, Logarithms, the Trigonometric functions and many other "intrinsic" or "library" functions is covered in detail in the main body of *Learning Level II*.

The Chapter is not without value, however, even though Level II has outdated much of it. If you need experience in calling complex subroutines, and want to have subroutines call other subroutines, then you can learn from the Chapter. We are leaving it in its original Level I form . . . so you will have to convert the Level I shorthand and error messages for yourself.

Changes in Chapter 26

☑Page 165, change the first two lines to:

By now, the Computer has given you plenty of nasty messages. You know something's wrong, but it isn't always obvious exactly where, or why.

☑Page 165, in the bottom 5 lines the number 3583 appears three times. Change it to **15572** in all three places.

☑Page 165, cross out the top shaded area. Change the second shaded area to read:

or **738∅** (8K machine) ;**3284 (4K)**.

☑Page 166, lines 1∅ thru 18 should be changed to read:

Type (very carefully):

```
5 DIM A (3835)

1∅ FORX=1TO3835:A(X)=X:NEXTX:FORY=
                 1TO3835:PRINTA(Y);

2∅ IFA(Y) -A(Y-1)<>1PRINT"BAD"

3∅ NEXTY
```

Then, RUN

After a **short** wait for the array to "spin-up", the monitor should display

1 2 3 4 5 6 7 8 (etc., through **3835**)

☑Page 166, the 4th shaded area, change to:

For 8K of memory, use **1787** instead of **3835** in Line **5** and **1∅**; for **4K**, use **764**.

☑ Page 166, the 5th shaded area, change to:

    . . . or **1787** . . . or **764**

☑ Page 167, delete the third shaded area and from line 2∅ to the end of the page.

☑ Page 168, delete the first shaded area and lines 1 thru 7.

☑ Page 168, item 1.b. should read:

    1b. Use an **illegal** variable name?

    Example:

    `1∅ INPUT 6G`

    ERROR: **Variable names must be recognizable by the Computer.**

☑ Page 168, 7 lines up from the bottom, change to:

    number larger than **65529?**

☑ Page 169, change the first line to:

    f. Type a line more than **255** characters long?

☑ Page 169, change line 1∅ to:

    `2∅ DATA 2,5`

        (Note deletion of second comma)

☑ Page 17∅, items 5 and 6, change to:

5. The error comes back as **?OM (out of memory)** but the **PRINT MEM** indicates there is room left in memory. If you get an **?OM** and are using the A(X) numeric array, **extra room (up to hundreds of bytes) has to be left for processing.** You have probably overrun the amount of available memory.

6. The ERROR comes back as **?BS (Subscript out of range).**
a. Did you exceed the limits of one of the built-in functions?
b. Did one of the values on the line exceed the maximum or minimum size for Level **II** numbers?

☑ Page 171, delete line numbers 19 and 2∅.

PART C
Level I
Some User's Programs

These user's programs were written especially for the Level I TRS-80, but will also RUN at Level II. Virtually all require slight modification, but the main one is simple conversion from "shorthand" to regular BASIC. You already know how to do this with the aid of the table on the inside back cover of the Level I Manual.

Far and away the most treacherous conversion is from PRINT AT to PRINT@. Watch very carefully that:

1. you do NOT use SHIFT@ in place of just plain @, and

2. that the @ is followed by a comma, not a semicolon.

Certain other modifications are more complex, such as changing the timing loops. Some modifications eliminate complex subroutines and use intrinsic functions instead. The following pages give you new program lines with the logic or syntax changes incorporated to make every program RUN on your Level II machine.

Test Grader Program

```
37Ø DATA 5,3,2,5,1,2,4,3,1,4
```

Slowpoke

Change line 2 to read:

puter says "G", you press **BREAK** to stop it. Then it's the next player's turn to

No program line changes are necessary.

12 – Hour Clock

```
7Ø FOR N = 1 TO 265
```

Checksum For Business

In program line 17Ø, delete the comma at the very end.

Design Program For
Cubical Quad Antenna

This program runs as is. It can be speeded up a bit by removing the square root subroutine starting with line 1ØØØØ and working SQR into the program at those places which call the subroutine.

Since we haven't studied SQR yet, making that conversion is an optional assignment for students who may already know how to use it.

Speed Reading

```
2Ø B=(12*6Ø/W) *   35Ø

3Ø REM 35Ø = FOR/NEXT LOOPS IN ONE SECOND
```

The Wheel Of Fortune

```
5 DIM A(6Ø)
```

Dow-Jones Industrial Average Forecaster

```
1ØØ INPUT A$

11Ø IF A$ = "Y" THEN 27Ø
```

On A Snowy Evening . . .

No logic or syntax changes required.

Triple check your PRINT@'s

Termites

No logic or syntax changes required.

Triple check your PRINT@s.

Sorry

```
5 DIM A(45)

59Ø FOR T = 1 TO 1ØØØ : NEXT T : FOR X = 1 TO 4
```

In lines 5ØØ and 55Ø, the arrows are supposed to be made up of less than or greater than signs and equal signs, thus:

```
<<<===<<<
```

Automatic Ticket Number Drawer

Add or change these lines:

```
22Ø A(N) = RND(E)

23Ø FOR S = Ø TO N-1

24Ø IF A(N) = A(S) GOTO 22Ø

262 PRINTTAB(12);">----->>> ";A(N) + B - 1
```

At Level II, the program will work for up to 1Ø winners. For more than that it is necessary to add a DIMension line. For up to 25 winners, add:

```
6 DIM A(25)
```

Craps

Add or change these lines:

```
1ØØ PRINT,,"YOUR POINT IS";N : GOTO 13Ø

11Ø PRINT,,"YOU WIN!!" : PRINT : END

12Ø PRINT,,"YOU LOSE." : PRINT : END
```

Fire When Ready, Gridley

Delete line 182Ø

Change:

```
181Ø CLS : GOTO 1Ø
```

House Security

Make the following changes::

```
2Ø PRINT"ANSWER EACH QUESTION WITH A NUMBER.
                      (1 = YES Ø = NO)"

8Ø IF (A=1)*(B=1)*(C=1)*(D=1)*(E=1) THEN 12Ø
```

Loan Amortization

Make these changes:

```
14Ø PRINT Z; : PRINTTAB(1Ø);P : PRINTTAB(2Ø);M;

15Ø PRINTTAB(3Ø);B; : PRINTTAB(4Ø);A
```

APPENDIX A
Level I
Subroutines

Nearly all these subroutines are found in Level II as intrinsic or library functions. Those that are not can be derived by simpler means.

Specifically:

ArcCosine

```
ARCCOS(X) = -ATN(X/SQR(-X*X+1))
```

ArcSine

```
ARCSIN(X) = ATN(X/SQR(-X*X+1))
```

APPENDIX B

Level I Manual

Cassette Data Files

Page 221, change program line 1ØØ to

```
1ØØPRINT #-1,A,B,C
```

Page 221, delete lines 1Ø, 11 and 12 up from the bottom.

Page 222, lines 2, 3 and 4 apply only if you are not using the CTR-80 recorder, designed specifically to overcome this and similar-type weaknesses. If you don't have a CTR-80, you might see the article in the April 1978 issue of *KiloBaud* magazine, written by Lien and Waterman. It shows how to build an inexpensive control box to greatly simplify controlling the recorder, and eliminate ground loops as well.

Page 222, change program lines as follows

    1ØØ (delete, unnecessary)

```
11Ø INPUT #-1,A,B,C
```

Page 222, delete the shaded area and lines 17 and 18.

Page 223, change line 4 to read:

lock-up condition described above, or getting an OD error message.

Page 223, change these program lines:

```
8Ø INPUT #-1,Y,Z

22Ø PRINT #-1,T,H
```

Page 223, 4th line from the bottom should begin

Line 8Ø (instead of 7Ø)

Last line should begin

Line 22Ø (instead of 21Ø)

NOTE: While this program (as modified above) does demonstrate the point of the chapter, the same program in greatly expanded form is printed next. It is much easier to follow. We will be using and modifying it later in *Learning Level II* for learning how to use twin cassettes. It is printed on the facing page in case you wish to substitute it for the program on page 223, and save it on tape for our later use.

```
10 REM   * TEMPERATURE AND HUMIDITY RECORDING PROGRAM *
20 REM   * DATA STORAGE MUST START ON THE 1ST DAY OF MONTH *
40 CLS : INPUT"WHAT DAY OF THE MONTH IS IT";D
50 INPUT"WHAT IS TODAYS TEMPERATURE";T
60 INPUT"WHAT IS TODAYS HUMIDITY";H
70 PRINT:PRINT
80 IF D = 1 GOTO 430            ' ON FIRST DAY IS NO PRIOR DATA
100 REM  * INPUTTING DATA STORED ON CASSETTE TAPE *
110 PRINT"WE MUST LOAD PRIOR DAYS TEMP & HUMIDITY FROM"
120 PRINT"THE DATA TAPE. BE SURE IT'S REWOUND AND THE RECORDER"
130 PRINT"IS SET TO 'PLAY'." : PRINT : PRINT
140 INPUT"PRESS 'ENTER' WHEN EVERYTHING IS READY TO GO. ";A$
160 CLS:PRINT"DATA IS NOW FLOWING INTO THE COMPUTER FROM TAPE."
170 PRINT : PRINT : PRINT"DATE","TEMP","HUMIDITY" : PRINT
180 FOR X = 1 TO D-1
190 INPUT #-1,Y,Z               ' BRINGS IT IN FROM TAPE
195 PRINT X,Y,Z                 ' PRINTS IT ON THE SCREEN
200 B = B+Y : C = C+Z           ' KEEPS RUNNING TOTALS
210 NEXT X
300 REM  * MONTHS AVERAGES TO-DATE *
310 B = (B+T)/D : C = (C+H)/D         ' COMPUTES THE AVERAGES
320 PRINT D,T,H
330 PRINT : PRINT "    **    THIS MONTHS AVERAGES   **"
340 PRINTTAB(7);"TEMP";TAB(17);"HUMIDITY"
350 PRINTTAB(7);B;TAB(19);C
400 REM  * STORING TODAYS TEMP & HUMIDITY ON TAPE *
410 PRINT:PRINT:INPUT"PRESS 'ENTER' WHEN READY TO CONTINUE";A$
420 CLS : PRINT : PRINT
430 PRINT"TODAYS TEMPERATURE AND HUMIDITY WILL NOW BE PRINTED"
440 PRINT"ON THE DATA TAPE. BE SURE 'RECORD' & 'PLAY' ARE"
450 PRINT"PRESSED. DO NOT REWIND THE TAPE, YET." : PRINT
460 INPUT"WHEN ALL IS READY, PRESS 'ENTER'";A$ : CLS
470 PRINT"TODAYS DATA IS NOW FLOWING FROM THE COMPUTER TO THE"
480 PRINT"TAPE. WE WILL INPUT THIS PLUS THE EARLIER DATA "
490 PRINT"TOMORROW." : PRINT
500 PRINT #-1,T,H                       ' PRINTS TODAY ON TAPE
520 PRINT"TODAYS NUMBERS HAVE BEEN ADDED TO THE TAPE."
530 PRINT"REWIND THE TAPE IN PREPARATION FOR TOMORROW."
```

APPENDIX C

Level I

Combined Function and ROM TEST

This factory test program was designed to check out Level I machines. It is a valuable program, but we must bear in mind that it checks only the functions we have learned SO FAR. The RAM test and display checkout are much more thorough than the short one we learned earlier.

Page 225 and 227. Change the program lines indicated:

```
15 CLS:PRINT@Ø,"TRS-80 LEVEL I FUNCTION TEST"

29Ø CLS:PRINT"LEVEL I FUNCTIONS ARE OK.
            THE RAM TEST IS NOW RUNNING."

30Ø A = MEM/4 - 35 : B=Ø, INCREASE THE 35 AS NEEDED

41Ø A$ = "GH"

47Ø PRINT@896

48Ø FOR X=1 TO 3Ø : PRINT A$; : NEXT X

5ØØ IF K>Ø A$="8Ø"

51Ø IF K<Ø A$="GH"
```

Delete program lines 44Ø and 45Ø.

If an OM error message is received in the vicinity of 3ØØ-35Ø, it will be necessary to change the "35" in line 3ØØ to adjust the "head space".

TECHNICAL SPECIFICATIONS

Level I

Pin Connections

Page 228, under Pin Connections for Expansion - Port Edge Card

In all but the earliest models of the TRS-80, pin connector #39 at the expansion port has been grounded. Therefore, there is no longer a way to obtain 5 volts from the edge card to power external devices.

P/N 39 should be changed to read:

39   GND   Signal Ground

Part II

New Power at the Command Level

Level II Overview

Now that we've been through "introductory" BASIC we can get serious about "intermediate" BASIC, called Level II. This is a sort of "catch up" and "catch all" Chapter, showing you a lot of little features of Level II BASIC that didn't find a home in the *Level I User's Manual.* Read each of them, do the sample programs and think about them. Each will fall into place in the chapters which follow.

Variable Names

We know we can use the 26 letters of the alphabet as names for variables. In Level II we can also use the numbers $\emptyset$ through 9 in conjunction with these letters:

A3 = 65

F9 = 37

      etc.

Instead of having just the 26 letter variables (which in reality is usually enough) the numbers give us an additional 26 * 1$\emptyset$= 26$\emptyset$. They can be very handy, particularly if we want to label a number of "sub" variables (D1, D2, D3, etc.) which combine to make a grand total which we just call D.

In addition, we can use *almost* any two-**letter** combination for a name. For example:

PI = 3.14159

C = PI * D   circumference = 3.14159 * diameter

Now that really looks valuable.

This feature gives us another 26 * 26 variables, and if that isn't enough to solve all your problems, nothing will. Nearly a thousand possible variable names so far, and we'll discover several times that many before we're through.

Enter this program and RUN, watching for an error message:

```
1 CLS : PRINT

1Ø RATE = 55

2Ø TIME = 3

3Ø DISTANCE = RATE * TIME

4Ø PRINT RATE, TIME, DISTANCE

9Ø PRINT : LIST
```

?SN got us in line 3Ø. The word DISTANCE is too long. Let's cut it back to DISTA and RUN again.

OK, that got us past line 3Ø, but the same problem exists in 4Ø. Cut DISTANCE back to 5 characters and try again.

That's more like it. Looks pretty good doesn't it. We can actually use words to name our variables. Add this line and RUN:

```
35 DIME = 1Ø
```

Another SN error? What's wrong with DIME???

It just so happens that the word DIM (dimension) is only one of a mess of "reserved" words, and we can't use them in variable names for obvious reasons. DIM is the first 3 letters of DIME.

Many of these words are not reserved for Level II BASIC, but for "Advanced" BASIC as used in the DISK system (TRSDOS). The result is the same — we can't use them. Appendix C contains the list of reserved words. (Better take a look now . . . there's big trouble ahead if you don't. *A word to the wise.)*

Okay, how about just cutting back 2 letters. We know we can use *almost* **any** 2 letter combination for a name. Try: ON TO IF and OR (won't work). GO and OF work even tho reserved.

Now try:

        35 DI = 1Ø

                and RUN.

It ran, but look at the answer! DISTA was printed as 1Ø instead of 165. What happened? DISTA surely can't be the same as DI. Well, it might look different, but the Computer only sees the first 2 letters, and they **are** the same. The DI in line 35 gave the DI in DISTA a new value.

The lesson here should be pretty clear. It's very easy to get all carried away with fancy variable names, and in the process find lots of trouble. Remember KISS? (**K**eep **I**t **S**imple, **S**tupid!)

New String Variables

In addition to the new variables we've discovered so far, we have **all** the letters of the alphabet available for strings, not just A$ and B$. And the numbers Ø through 9 too, plus any 2 letter combination. These are all valid string names:

X$

D8$

PI$

   etc.

Almost another thousand variable names.

Array Names

Same thing? Yep.

A(N)

BC(N)

D3(N)

E4$(N)

XY$(N)

   are all legal array names. The last 2 deal with "string arrays." We've devoted an entire Chapter later to the expanded capabilities of arrays.

Shorthand

You of course know that old Level I Shorthand is no more, having made way for other good things. There are several little "shorthand" tricks that we can use, however.

The first is the use of ? in place of the very common word, PRINT. Type this line:

```
10 ?"QUESTION MARK"
```

and LIST it. Awwk! The pumpkin turned into a coach. The Computer rewrote it to read:

```
10 PRINT"QUESTION MARK"
```

It also works at the command level. Try:

```
>?3*R   and we get
```

```
12
```

If you have the numeric keyboard you'll especially appreciate this feature since the same upper-case characters are available above the pad numbers as above the keyboard ones. They just aren't marked. Try it.

The value of this is, a touch typist can type ?" with the right hand, while the left hand holds down the left SHIFT key, considerably speeding up the typing of PRINT lines.

The ' is shorthand for REM, and is especially nice when documenting the purpose of a line. It makes program lines into multiple statement lines. ' = :REM.

```
50  X = Z*C/4 +33                    ' THE SECRET
                                       EQUATION
```

The only place it can't be used unaided is in a DATA line, and that problem can be overcome by actually adding a : to the DATA line. See lines 1000 and 1010 in this program.

```
10 REM   * SEVERE WEATHER ALERT SYMBOL AS SEEN ON KELO-TV *
20                  ' H = HORIZONTAL STARTING POSITION
30                  ' V = VERTICAL STARTING POSITION
40 CLS              ' N = NUMBER OF VERTICAL BLOCKS TO BE SET
50 READ H,V,N  :  V1 = V      ' READ DATA & STORE V FOR RECALL
60 IF N = 0 GOTO 60           ' LOCKING LOOP WHEN OUT OF DATA
70  FOR H = H TO H+2          ' 3 PASSES FOR TRIPLE BLOCK WIDTH
80    FOR V = V TO V+N-1      ' COUNTS PRINTING OF N BLOCKS
90     SET(H,V) : NEXT V      ' SETS LIGHT BLOCKS & CLOSES LOOP
100 V=V1 : NEXT H : GOTO50    ' RESETS V TO DATA LINE VALUE
1000 DATA 102,3,9, 105,10,1, 108,7,3, 111,6,1  : ' DATA IS IN-
1010 DATA 114,7,3, 117,10,1, 120,3,9, 0,0,0    : ' H,V,N, ORDER
```

The Period . is of minimal value as a BASIC shorthand word, but if you've just typed a new line, listed one, or Edited one (next chapter), you can repeat it without typing its number by:

90 REM TEST LINE   **ENTER**

then type

LIST

and line 90 will be LISTed. This works even if the program has been RUN, which can be an aid if you are troubleshooting a line and don't want to write down its number. It also works with a line that keeps popping up due to an error message.

The ENTER Key

If you're the very observant type you will have noticed that program execution begins when the **ENTER** key is **pressed.** At Level I, it began when the **ENTER** key was **released.** Try it on the resident program. This becomes important later on when we're doing such precision things as setting the Real Time Clock.

Special Keys

The keyboard is pretty self-explanatory, but there are several keys we've not used yet.

RIGHT ARROW is used as preset TAB. Go ahead and press it a few times. It TABs over in increments of 8, starting with 0, following a 0, 8, 16, etc. sequence. Is helpful when typing a program and you know exactly where you are going and can indent accordingly.

A **SHIFT** RIGHT ARROW converts the screen display from
64 characters to 32 characters. Try it. The CLEAR key
clears the screen and returns printing to 64 characters
per line.

LEFT ARROW is for people who change their mind a lot.
You've already used it for correcting errors, one at a
time. By pressing the **shift** key at the same time, you
can wipe out the entire line you just typed.

UP ARROW will be studied in the next 2 chapters.

DOWN ARROW is also called the "linefeed". It moves the
cursor down to the next line. Its use will be studied in a
later chapter.

NOT

In addition to the logical AND and OR functions, we now
have what is called logical NOT. Here is how it can be used:
Type:

```
1 CLS : PRINT

1Ø INPUT"ENTER A NUMBER";N

2Ø L = NOT(N>5)

3Ø IF L = Ø GOTO 5Ø

4Ø PRINT "N WAS NOT GREATER THAN 5" :
                      PRINT : LIST

5Ø PRINT "N WAS GREATER THAN 5" : PRINT : LIST
```

and RUN.

Line 2Ø is obviously the key one, containing NOT. If the
statement in line 2Ø is **true** (namely, that N is NOT larger
than 5) the Computer says the statement is false and makes
the value of L = −1. The test in line 3Ø then fails.

If, on the other hand, L is larger than 5, it's because N is larger than 5, the statement is false and the Computer makes the value of L = $\emptyset$. True = -1 and False = $\emptyset$. It's just an extension of the "logical" math we learned in the Level I book. (Time for the primal scream, again. All together, now . . .)

Order of Operations

When trying to figure out which gets calculated first in the thick of your "humongous" equation, here's the pecking order:

Those operations buried deepest inside the parenthesis get resolved first. The idea is to clear the parenthesis as quickly as possible. When it all becomes a big tie, here's the order:

1. Exponentation — a number raised to a power (studied in a later chapter).
2. Negation, that is, a number having its sign changed. Typically, a number multiplied times -1.
3. Multiplication, then division: from left to right.
4. Addition, then subtraction: from left to right.
5. Less than, greater than, equals, less or equal to, greater or equal to, not equal to: from left to right.
6. The logical NOT
7. The logical AND
8. The logical OR

Use of Quotes & Semicolons

Technically, it is not necessary to use quotes to close off
many PRINT statements, like:

```
1Ø PRINT"WHERE IS THE END QUOTE?
```

RUNs just fine. Leave it off at your own peril.

Also, semicolons are not absolutely necessary to separate a
TAB number and the opening quote marks:

```
1Ø PRINTAB(1Ø) "OOPS, WE MISSED A SEMICOLON"
```

RUNs just fine. Leave it off at your own peril.

An interpreter that is "too forgiving" is like an airplane that
is "too forgiving." It allows you to become sloppy, and when
you really need all the skill you can muster, it is gone from
the lack of practice imposed by its discipline. You are
strongly encouraged not to take these and other "cheap"
short-cuts.

INPUT??

When INPUTting several variables in a single INPUT line, if
you fail to input them all, separated by commas, the special
prompt, ?? alerts you to the fact that more DATA must be
INPUT. Enter this program and enter only one number at a
time, followed by **ENTER** . Watch for the ?? :

```
1Ø INPUT A,B,C
```

and RUN

RUN it again and try to INPUT a letter instead of a number.
It responds with

```
?REDO
```

There is extensive information in the Appendix dealing with Error Messages. REDO is reminding you that you can't INPUT a string variable into a request for a numeric one.

YES and NO

At Level I (uncorrected for Level II) we had a unique way to set up the program to receive Y and N responses. It was nice but definitely not part of mainline BASIC. The old timers will remember:

```
1Ø  Y=1  :  N=Ø
```

and away we went.

This is strictly verboten at Level II. (Try it if you don't believe.) Very soon we have a series of chapters dealing with Strings, and there we learn the "standard" way to INPUT for YES and NO responses.

Optional NEXT

FOR-NEXT loops don't always have to specify which FOR you are NEXTing. This can be useful when the loops are nested.

Type this program:

```
1Ø  FOR N = 1 TO 5 : PRINT N

2Ø    FOR Q = 1 TO 3 : PRINT ,Q

3Ø      FOR R = 1 TO 4 : PRINT ,,R

4Ø NEXT : NEXT : NEXT
```

For safety, in loops which can be broken out of with IF-THEN tests, it is wise to be specific.

An alternate way to be specific is:

```
4Ø  NEXT R,Q,N
```

225 Characters per line

Level II permits up to 255 characters in a single program line
— 4 screen widths of 64 characters each. (Don't ask **me** to
debug such a line!).

IF-THEN-ELSE

ELSE is an interesting addition to our stable of conditional
branching statements. It allows us an option other than dropping to the next line if a test fails. Try this one:

```
1 CLS : PRINT

1Ø INPUT "ENTER A NUMBER";N

2Ø IF N=Ø PRINT "ZERO" ELSE PRINT
                        "NOT ZERO"

3Ø PRINT : LIST
```

and RUN.

Optional THEN

Both THEN and GOTO are optional in expressions which do not require GOing to a line number if the test passes. This can be useful in long PRINT lines, where PRINTing is the result if the test passes.

```
1Ø IF X = Ø PRINT "X = Ø"          (works)
```

but

```
1Ø IF X = Ø 1ØØ              (does not work)
```

```
99 END
```

```
1ØØ PRINT "1ØØ HERE"
```

Line 1Ø must read either:

```
1Ø IF X = Ø THEN 1ØØ
```

or

```
1Ø IF X = Ø GOTO 1ØØ
```

TABbing

The TAB function can handle numbers up through 255. This has no value in displays printed on the tube, but on big line printers it is common to have PRINT widths up to 132 characters.

POS(N)

A new and sometimes useful statement allows the Computer to report back the position of the cursor. This simple program tells all:

```
1 CLS : PRINT

1Ø INPUT"ENTER A NUMBER BETWEEN -1Ø
                       AND 53";A

2Ø PRINT TAB(1Ø + A)

3Ø PRINT POS(N)

4Ø PRINT"WAS THE NUMBER OF THE NEXT
                  PRINT POSITION"

9Ø PRINT : LIST
```

        and RUN.

Line 3Ø is the key one, containing POS. The N inside brackets is just a "dummy". Most anything else would have worked as well — but something has to be placed there. POS reports back any cursor position up thru 63. Numbers beyond that start over again with zero, as you will find if you enter a number larger than 53 in the above program.

CLOAD?

At Level II we are able to check a program on tape against the one in memory. That way we can be sure of getting a good "load" before erasing the memory. (Won't **that** relieve some acid indigestion?)

After doing a CSAVE"A", rewind the tape. Set it up to play, and type:

>   CLOAD?"A"

>   and RUN.

Watch the blinking asterisks. It looks like we are loading in a program, but are actually just comparing it, character for character, against what's already there. We are not erasing or changing the memory. If they don't match up for any reason, the test will stop and the screen read

>   BAD

"BAD" means we'd better CSAVE the program again, maybe on a different tape.

If we type just

>   CLOAD?

without specifying the name of the program, it will check the first program on the tape against memory, and that's normally all we want to do.

NOTES

The Editor

An extraordinarily valuable capability of Level II is a feature called the **EDITOR**. Its purpose is as simple as its name. It lets you "EDIT", or make changes in a program. The Level II TRS-80 uses a so-called "line editor" since it edits letters and numbers in only one line at a time. It is so easy to use but so powerful you'll never again want to use a computer without one.

Type in this line (errors and all):

```
1Ø PRINT "THIS HEAR ARE SHORE A FLOXY
                         CONFUSER."
```

and RUN

"CONFUSER? YEP! THAT SHORE IS A GOOD NAME FER IT!"

It should RUN just fine, and if that's the way you usually talk you're probably wondering what all the fuss is about. If, on the other hand, you wish to change the sentence to something like

```
THIS SURE IS A FOXY COMPUTER.
```

then we need to do some EDITing in line 1Ø.

Now in the "old days" with Level I, we would have to retype the entire line, hoping we didn't make more mistakes than we eliminated. This particular example has so much to change it might be just as easy to retype it, but our purpose is to "exercise" the editor, so type:

```
EDIT 1Ø
```

and see what happens.

Hokay . . . we get

10_

a good (but not perfect) sign it's in the EDITOR mode.

We know from studying the "changes" part of *Learning Level II* that to get out of this situation we could just hit **ENTER** . Being in EDITOR isn't like being in BASIC. We only use **ENTER** when we are **done** EDITing and want to **return** to BASIC. The EDITOR is **not** part of BASIC. It's a special feature we call up from BASIC using the word EDIT.

Hit the L Key.

The screen now shows:

10 PRINT "THIS HEAR IS SHORE A FLOXY CONFUSER."

10_

By Typing L we LISTed the line being edited. Then the cursor returned back where we started — still in EDITOR.

Since we want line 10 to read THIS SURE IS A FOXY COMPUTER, let's first get rid of the word HEAR. Tap the space bar slowly and watch it print one new character each time. After you get to

10 PRINT "THIS_

press the letter D (which stands for DELETE) *5 times.* It will add to the screen:

! !!H!!E!!A!!R!

Between each pair of exclamation marks is the letter or space which was DELETED. Press L again and let's list the line and see what it looks like now. But pressing L once just LISTs the rest of the line. Pressing it a second time lists the entire line as it now exists after EDITing. Shore enuf, the word "HEAR" and the space which preceded it are gone.

By the way, here are 2 additional ways to space forward and backward — while still in the EDIT mode.

1. To space forward 5 spaces (or other number), you can type 5 and then press the space bar.

2. To BACKspace 5 spaces (or other number), you can type 5 ← .

Let's now change the word ARE to IS, and learn another EDITing trick in the process. The EDIT letter S stands for SEARCH. Instead of using the space bar and tapping over to the A in ARE, let's let the Computer SEARCH for the letter A. As we look at line 1Ø from left to right, we see that the A in ARE is the first A in the line, so type:

    SA   (meaning, search for the first A)

and

    1Ø PRINT "THIS_

is displayed

Now we just learned that we can get rid of ARE by typing D (for DELETE) 3 times in a row, but it's quicker and easier to just type

    4D   (do it) it means "delete the next 4 characters".
         (ARE *and the space following it*)

The line now reads

    1Ø PRINT"THIS !ARE !_

Let's type a couple of L's to see what we have now:

    1Ø PRINT"THIS SHORE A FLOXY CONFUSER."

We know we have to insert the word IS between THIS and SHORE. Worded another way, we have to insert a new word between the first two S's. Any ideas? How about SEARCHing for the 2nd S? We won't print it — just search for it.

Type

2SS (search for the 2nd S)

and the screen reads

1Ø PRINT"THIS_

Now we can use the INSERT feature. Very carefully, and **only once** (since nothing will show on the screen), type I.

You have activated INSERT. Type the letters

IS

and press the space bar once

The screen now reads

1Ø PRINT"THIS IS _

We've inserted the IS and a space following it, but must now **leave** the INSERT mode. We can always completely bail out of the EDITor at any time by hitting **ENTER**, but since we have a lot more work to do on this line, we instead press **SHIFT** and the up-arrow ↑ key at the same time. As with pressing I, nothing shows on the screen. Now press L to see what we've got left.

1Ø PRINT "THIS IS SHORE A FLOXY CONFUSER."

1Ø_

If it seems like we're going slowly, you're right! The EDITOR is so important but so simple we may as well learn it right the first time. You know the old story, "there's never time to do it right the first time, but always time to do it over."

Forging onward ... let's use the next feature called C (for CHANGE, or exchange). We can change the word SHORE to SURE by DELETing the H and CHANGING the O to a U. So, let's type

2SH   to SEARCH for the 2nd H

10 PRINT "THIS IS S_

and D to DELETE it.

Very carefully, type a single

C   (it will not show on the screen)

This permits us to change the next letter to some other letter or character. Type

U

and then

L   twice to get a fresh new line to see what's left.

10 PRINT"THIS IS SURE A FLOXY CONFUSER."

Think for a moment. How can we change FLOXY to FOXY?

How about

SL   to SEARCH for the first L, then

D   to DELETE it, then

L   twice to see what the line now looks like.

10 PRINT"THIS IS SURE A FOXY CONFUSER."

10 _

Only one more word to change. Should we go into the word CONFUSER and DELETE the N & F and insert P & U? Would it be easier to just CHANGE those letters instead? What about the S? Think about it.

Of course! It takes fewer steps to CHANGE than to DELETE and then INSERT, so we always CHANGE when possible. Perform this sequence:

2SN	Search for the second N (the first one is in PRINT)
2C	prepare to CHANGE the next 2 letters
MP	the 2 new letters
SS	SEARCH for the next S
C	prepare to CHANGE one letter
T	the new letter
L	finish listing the line so we can look at it.

Whew! Finally done. But wait — we're still in EDITOR. Press **ENTER** , see the prompt, and know that we're back in BASIC. RUN it to be sure.

Despite our taking each editing task one step at a time, it is possible to make all these EDITing changes in only one pass through the line. The purpose of an editor *is to save time.*

Since you're now the "ace of the base" when it comes to flying this EDITOR, let's type

    NEW

and type in old line 1∅ again, then EDIT it in one pass.

    1∅ PRINT"THIS HEAR ARE SHORE A FLOXY CONFUSER."

Follow with me now, step by step. If you blow it, start all over by retyping line 1∅.

    >EDIT1∅   **ENTER**

L   to LIST it

2SH   SEARCH for 2nd H

8D   DELETE next 8 characters

I   prepare for INSERT

IS   the new letters

SHIFT ↑ terminate INSERT

SH   SEARCH for next H

D   DELETE next character

C   CHANGE next character

U   the new character

SL   SEARCH for the next L

D   DELETE it

SN   SEARCH for the next N

2C   CHANGE next 2 characters

MP   the new characters

SS   SEARCH for the next S

C   CHANGE next character

T   the new character

LL   to LIST the edited program for inspection

ENTER to leave the EDITor mode.

Pretty slick, huh? With some practice it will take you less than 3∅ seconds. From here on, you should always use the EDITOR for changes, especially in long lines. Compare the time it would take to change only one letter or number in a very long line by retyping that line, with the speed of doing it with the EDITOR.

"I CAN APPRECIATE YOUR ABILITY TO EDIT YOUR COMPUTER PROGRAMS BUT CAN YOU LEAVE THE NEWSPAPER ALONE UNTIL AFTER I READ IT?"

CHAPTER 3

The Editor — Second Semester

You could probably live happily ever after thinking you were in fat city with what you learned in the previous chapter, but the **EDITOR** has a number of other features which are handy to use when the occasion arises. One which will certainly arise is typified by the following lines. Erase the memory and type:

    1Ø PRIMT "THAT ISN'T HOW YOU SPELL PRINT"
    (NOTE: PRIMT is deliberately misspelled)

and RUN

    ?SN ERROR IN 1Ø

    READY

    1Ø _

means there is a syntax error in line 1Ø. The Computer is telling us *WHAT? — I don't understand what you are saying* **and automatically** putting us in the EDITOR mode at the line which contains the error. This always happens in Level II when there is a syntax error. (More on Syntax and other errors in the next chapter.) Meanwhile, proceed normally by typing:

L   to list the line

SM   to find the first M

CN   to CHANGE it to an N

L   to list for final look

<kbd>ENTER</kbd> to return to BASIC

While we're at it, let's examine another simple but sometimes troublesome point. Let's go back into EDIT and find the first P in the program.

```
EDIT 1Ø

SP
```

          what happened . . .?

Isn't the first P in the word PRINT? Yes, but when the Computer starts out in the EDIT mode, the cursor positions itself in place of the **first letter** of the **first word**, so it was **already** at the first P. Our SP searched out the NEXT P, which was in SPELL. Now you know.

There is a third and often convenient way to enter EDIT, particularly when experimenting and changing a value over and over in the same line. Type in this program:

```
1Ø REM * TESTING EDIT. *

2Ø FOR N = 1 TO 4ØØ : NEXT N

99 END
```

Now let's suppose we are trying to experimentally determine how many FOR-NEXT loops our specific computer must go thru to burn up exactly one second. We know it's somewhere around 4ØØ, but will have to "cut and try" with different numbers many times, checking against a stopwatch to really get close.

RUN the program first, then

```
EDIT 2Ø
```
and change the 4ØØ to any other number and RUN again.

To get back into the EDITOR to change line 2Ø again it is not necessary to EDIT 2Ø again. The Computer remembers which line you last EDITed. Simply type

```
EDIT.(the . means "the last line edited")
```

This nice feature, while convenient, is a bit squirrelly. If you type a LIST, RUN more than once, or do any of a number of normal things, the Computer forgets where you last EDITed. It sort of runs out of steam at that point and throws you into EDIT at the last line of the program. Type:

LIST **ENTER**

then

EDIT. **ENTER**

and you'll see.

99 _

Q if for Quit (without changes)

We know that whenever we type RUN, all values are initialized to zero, but hold their last value **after** the RUN. It turns out that whenever we do an EDIT, the values are also reset to zero. This can be a disadvantage if we are in the process of troubleshooting and are automatically thrown into EDIT by a syntax error. Let's add a line to the resident program to demonstrate the point:

5∅ PRIMT N
(Note: PRIMT misspelling deliberate)

RUN the program and let it crash.

?SN ERROR IN 5∅

Don't make any changes in 5∅ at this time, but just exit the EDITOR by hitting **ENTER** .

Now check the value of N in memory by typing: PRINT N at the command level.

∅ is the value, indicating it has been initialized.

RUN the program again, crashing at 5∅ again, but exit the EDITOR by typing a simple:

Q   which stands for "quit without changes"

Then

> PRINT N   Shows its value to be
>
> 4Ø1   (or one more than the number you finally ended
>   up with for N)

This may not really be all that profound, but if you're chasing a real ornery bug and want to check the values of the variables before doing any EDITing, Q is the way to do it. A fast EDIT. will bring you back into EDITOR at the offending line without you even having to write down its number or having to remember it.

Q also lets you escape from EDIT if you change your mind and don't really want to make those changes you already did.

(E) is for END and EXIT

E is the opposite of Q. When you are satisfied with the changes, type E and you're back in BASIC. E does the same thing as hitting **ENTER**

(A) is for ABORT

If, after making some changes via the EDITOR and looking at them with an L you decide you don't want to make them, type an A. The changes, regardless how drastic, are not final until you exit the EDITOR, and A will kick them all out and let you start over again. Type L, following the A, to see what the original line looks like again.

> EDIT 2Ø
>> and make a few changes. Enter an A and then L to get the feel for it. Be sure if you enter INSERT that you exit it first or the A won't work.

K is for KILL

K is a combination of SEARCH AND DELETE, starting with the **beginning** of the line. Type:

EDIT 2Ø   then

KT   then

LL   to see what happened

It KILLED everything up to (but not including) the first T. "Take it all back" by typing an A, then L, then try:

2KN   then

LL   and see that everything up to the 2nd N was KILLED.

AL   to "take it all back"

H is for HACK

HACK is sort of the mirror image of KILL in that it DELETEs everything from the cursor **to the end** of the line. It just "hacks" off the end of the line, without showing it on the screen, AND goes into the INSERT mode. Nice if you need it, and great for "hackers".

If you don't need to go into the INSERT mode, the old traditional "99D", meaning DELETE the next 99 characters (which is usually more than enough to erase the rest of the line), is the best approach.

To implement HACK, SEARCH for the starting point, then H off the end of the line, and type the new ending in its place.

X is to eXtend

Suppose you wanted to go to the end of a line and add some more to it — to extend it. You can type X which also throws the EDITOR into INSERT. X is a one-step replacement for:

S   Which searches for the carriage return

I   Puts EDITOR into Insert

Give it a try on one of the program lines.

That's —30—

With steady but persistent practice, you will become very skillful at using the EDITOR. It will in turn reward you handsomely with great savings in time and frustration.

"IT SAYS SOMETHING HERE ABOUT A SYNTAX...
WHEN YOU COME TO THINK ABOUT IT, THEY'VE
TAXED JUST ABOUT EVERYTHING ELSE!"

" THOSE ARE TAXES THAT WILL REALLY KILL YOU!"

NOTES

CHAPTER 4
Chasing Bugs

We saw in the previous two Chapters that the EDITOR is a powerful aid in changing programs once we find out what is wrong. In this Chapter we will learn how to use the built-in diagnostic tools to help hunt down the actual errors.

TRON/TROFF

The simplicity but power of TRON/TROFF is awesome. Enter this program:

```
1Ø  FOR N = 1 TO 5

2Ø  PRINT "SEE TRON RUN"

3Ø  NEXT N

99  END
```

and RUN, to be sure it's OK.

Now, type TRON (which stands for TRacer ON), then RUN. The screen should say:

```
<1Ø><2Ø>SEE TRON RUN

<3Ø><2Ø>SEE TRON RUN

<3Ø><2Ø>SEE TRON RUN

<3Ø><2Ø>SEE TRON RUN

<3Ø><2Ø>SEE TRON RUN

<3Ø><99>
```

What does it mean?

The numbers between the **< >** are the program line numbers. TRON traces the sequence of program execution and prints each line number as it is "hit". How's that for powerful?

89

Now type TROFF (for TRacer OFF) and RUN.

The Tracing has stopped and

SEE TRON RUN

SEE TRON RUN

SEE TRON RUN

SEE TRON RUN

SEE TRON RUN

appears in the usual way. It's the very essence of simplicity.

Since TRON and TROFF can be used as program **statements** as well as commands, the possibilities for troubleshooting program *logic* are endless. Our little demonstration program is short and error-free, but by adding the following lines and RUNning, you will see another way tracing is used.

5 TRON

35 TROFF

Imagine its value in a program with dozens or hundreds of program lines all tangled up with IF-THEN's, ON-GOTO's, etc. The errors that will drive you wild are those you can't see. Although all characters appear to be upper-case on the screen, it ain't necessarily so. If you press the **SHIFT** key when typing a letter, the Computer will store it as a **lower-** case letter (just the opposite of a regular typewriter). The Computer has been trained to respond to both upper and lower case **letters** in many cases, as in the word PRINT.

Enter a 1Ø (line 1Ø) and then hold a **SHIFT** key down and type the rest of this line:

1Ø PRINT "HELLO THERE LOWER CASE"

and continue to hold **SHIFT** down while typing RUN.

Worked just fine, didn't it. We don't use those lower case letters for anything else anyway.

Now enter this program, but hold down the **SHIFT** key as you type the @.

```
1 CLS

1Ø PRINT@55Ø,"MISTAKE HERE"
```

and RUN.

Aha! The screen shows a plain old @ but the Computer doesn't recognize it, sends us an error message and throws us to the EDITOR.

An L displays a fine looking program line. Do a

S@   (**without** the **SHIFT** key)

and watch it SEARCH right over the @. Try again but hold down **SHIFT** . It snags it, and a simple

C@   (without **SHIFT**)

changes it to what we need. The above is a **very common** error since we use **SHIFT** @ so often to freeze listings and runs.

The EDITOR is a great tool to spot such errors, especially in very long lines where retyping would be tedious or hazardous. Simply step through the entire line SEARCHing for each character in turn. If you hit a lower-case character, the SEARCH will pass right over it, and you've found the bug. Try it! It really works.

Another nasty little invisible bug can be caused by hitting the down arrow (↓) key by accident when typing in a program line or when the EDITOR is in INSERT mode.

The result of either can be that parts of the program are scattered all over the screen. If severe enough, even a LISTing won't divulge the exact problem. Often the best solution is to just retype the offending line.

Clear the memory with NEW, then type

10 PRINT "DOWN ARROW▼ ▼ ▼ ▼ ▼ ▼DILEMMA"

and experiment with the down arrow in both AUTO and EDITOR modes and with and without the **SHIFT** key

As a little aside, the down arrow can be used to frustrate and slow down "program-peekers" who insist on LISTing your favorite program to find the secret formula.

Type in this program:

10 REM * SECRET EQUATION HIDER *

20 REM * THE NEXT LINE HAS THE EQUATION *

30 X=1234567890/987654321 + 1234567890 – 9876543210

(insert 16 down arrows before pressing **ENTER**)

40 PRINT"THE ANSWER IS";X

50 PRINT"MISSED THE SECRET FORMULA, DIDN'T YOU!"

99 END

and RUN

Then LIST. The LISTing at line 30 should whiz by so fast you can't read it. The only way to really freeze and analyze it is to first discover the line number which has the hidden arrows, then go into EDITOR there and step through each character one at a time. It's not at all foolproof, but slows the interloper down. Makes it even harder if you give the "secret" line an unusual line number that's harder to guess.

NOTES

CHAPTER 5

Chasing The Errors

In Level I there were only 3 error messages – WHAT, HOW and SORRY. WHAT worked pretty well, too, since it not only identified the line number containing the error, but often placed a question mark next to the offending character. When it came to HOW, however, some much stronger medicine was needed to help find those elusive errors.

Level II contains 23 different error messages. We'll list them for your reference. There are so many we need a separate chapter plus an Appendix just to understand what they mean.

Let's quietly tiptoe into the hall of errors by typing this little test program:

```
1 CLS

1Ø REM * TESTING ERROR CODES *

2Ø INPUT"WHAT ERROR CODE NUMBER SHALL WE CHECK";N

3Ø ERROR N
```

RUN the program a number of times, (entering numbers between 1 and 23), forcing the Computer to print out the abbreviation code for various types of errors. Don't waste time trying to understand them now. We will study them in detail in the next chapter.

The only new word above is in line 3Ø. ERROR has little real use in life except as above, printing the Error Code from its code number.

Further, Error Codes are not necessarily interchangeable between different interpreters. This is strictly an "in-house" thing, tho the principle of Error Codes is universal.

LEVEL II Error Codes

Code	Abbreviation	Error
1	NF	NEXT without FOR
2	SN	Syntax error
3	RG	Return without GOSUB
4	OD	Out of data
5	FC	Illegal function call
6	OV	Overflow
7	OM	Out of memory
8	UL	Undefined line
9	BS	Subscript out of range
10	DD	Redimensioned array
11	/O	Division by zero
12	ID	Illegal direct
13	TM	Type mismatch
14	OS	Out of string space
15	LS	String too long
16	ST	String formula too complex
17	CN	Can't continue
18	NR	NO RESUME
19	RW	RESUME without error
20	UE	Unprintable error
21	MO	Missing operand
22	FD	Bad file data
23	L3	Disk BASIC only

Error Trapping

The ON ERROR GOTO statement is of more value, and you should use it when you think you're on the trail of a specific type of error, but are not sure.

Suppose you suspect that someplace in the program there is an accidental division by zero, and it's goofing up the results. Type in this test program:

```
1Ø  ON ERROR GOTO 6Ø

2Ø  PRINT

3Ø  INPUT"WHAT NUMBER SHALL WE DIVIDE 1ØØ BY";N

4Ø  A = 1ØØ/N

5Ø  PRINT"1ØØ DIVIDED BY";N;"=";A

6Ø  GOTO 1Ø

7Ø  PRINT"DIVISION BY ZERO IS ILLEGAL - MAYBE
                           EVEN IMPOSSIBLE!"
```

IBM
100 ÷ Ø
= 1.701412E+38

and RUN. Try positive and negative values, then try Ø.

The ON ERROR GOTO is acting much as our old friend ON X GOTO did, so there are no big surprises here.

Remove line 1Ø and try assorted values, ending with Ø. Again, no big surprise. An error message was delivered pinpointing both the nature and location of the error, and execution was terminated with a READY.

Type line 1Ø back in

```
1Ø  ON ERROR GOTO 6Ø
```

and also add

```
8Ø  RESUME 2Ø
```

and RUN with various values, including Ø.

Notice that even tho the Computer was forced to operate with an error (division by zero), execution did not terminate. The error message was delivered and the Computer kept on going, thanks to RESUME. This is the essence of error trapping — identifying the error without "crashing" the program. There may be several interrelated errors that can be found easily only by continuing the RUN.

Change line 8∅ to

8∅ RESUME NEXT

      and RUN.

Tho the results are similar to those with RESUME 2∅, there is a subtle difference. RESUME NEXT causes execution to resume at the NEXT line immediately following the line which made the error. Thus line 5∅ gets printed, even tho (in this case) it gives a wrong answer. RESUME 2∅ directed execution to a very specific line. With a little head-scratching you can quickly see how both of these features can be used in difficult debugging situations.

Next, change line 8∅ to simply

8∅ RESUME

      and RUN.

As you see, RESUME by itself (or RESUME ∅) sends execution back to the line in which the error is being made. (If you are having difficulty visualizing what is taking place in any of these examples, just turn on TRON and it becomes as easy as following a road map.)

More variations on the theme

Change line 8Ø back to

   8Ø RESUME 2Ø

     and add line 75

75 PRINT"ERROR IS IN LINE #";ERL

     and RUN

ERL is a "reserved" word that prints the line number in which the error occurs. For my money, this little jewel in combination with ON ERROR GOTO to snag 'em, and RESUME NEXT to keep the program from crashing, makes this whole hassle worthwhile.

A final esoteric touch may be obtained by adding the ERR (not ERL) statement. ERR produces a number which when divided by 2 and increased by 1 (oh, swell) brings us back to the error code number. We've gone almost full cycle. Add line 77

   77 PRINT"AND ERROR CODE IS";ERR/2+1

     and RUN.

Finally, to complete this loop begun several pages ago, add

   78 PRINT"WHICH STANDS FOR" : ERROR ERR/2+1

     and RUN.

Which brings us back to DO, a deer, a female deer (it must be time to stop — getting too silly!).

We should note in passing that when using ERR, strange moonbeams sometimes affect the Computer. The interpreter temporarily takes on slightly different characteristics at the command level. We deliberately won't elaborate on them here as they don't seem harmful and will probably be ironed out in future versions of the interpreter. Just tho't it should be mentioned tho, lest you suspect the saucers have been flying again.

A very useful application of the error traps we've learned allows the program to automatically LIST the program if there is an error. It requires the addition of 2 temporary program lines using all 3 ERROR statements.

From Appendix A (which covers the Error messages) comes the example of what happens when there is an error in a FOR-NEXT loop. Type in:

```
1Ø FOR A = 1 TO 5

2Ø PRINT "THERE IS NO 'NEXT A'"

3Ø NEXT Z
```

   and RUN.

In this simple program the Computer responds with

```
?NF ERROR IN 3Ø.
```

There is a FOR-NEXT error in LINE 3Ø. By adding the following lines we can approximate the same result, plus cause an automatic program LISTing:

```
5 ON ERROR GOTO 1ØØ
```
   to 'set' the error trap

```
99 END
```
   to END execution if all is well

```
1ØØ PRINT ERL,ERR/2+1 : LIST
```
   to print the line # with the error, the error code (which can be found in Appendix A) and LIST the program (or LIST##-##).

Try this routine. If all is well in the program, nothing will seem different. If there is an error, it will be trapped as you can see on the screen.

Wow — just like *The BASIC Handbook!*

Appendix A contains the results of a lot of effort expended to help you understand what the 23 error messages really mean. It follows the style of *The BASIC Handbook* (by your friendly author) and is meant to be a high quality reference on TRS-80 Error Codes.

Tho readers traditionally do not read appendices, your assignment is do a Go-Sub to Appendix A and at least carefully skim its contents. Really serious students of the TRS-80 will take the time to make Appendix A a separate study lesson, going through each of the sample programs. An in-depth knowledge for these important diagnostic tools will pay dividends far beyond the time taken to understand them.

AUTOmatic Line Numbering

They Laughed When I Sat Down At The Computer To Play

As the artist approaches a blank canvass with only a gleam in his eye, so you approach your empty Computer and type:

    AUTO

        the screen returns

    1Ø _

Are we in EDITOR??? It looks like it! But we're not. We are in an AUTOmatic line numbering mode. Type:

    PRINT"WHAT IS GOING ON HERE?"

        and

    2Ø _

        pops up on the screen.

Type:

    PRINT"THIS IS RIDICULOUS."

        and

    3Ø _

        appears.

Well, it's obvious at this point that we're being fed the new line numbers as fast as we need them. Hit the **ENTER·** key a few more times and watch them jump. Okay — how do we get OUT of AUTO? Hit the **BREAK** key.

Type LIST and see that only those line numbers you actually used (1∅ and 2∅) contain anything.

Type NEW, then

```
AUTO 1∅∅∅,2∅∅
```

Hit the **ENTER** key a half dozen times or so and the pattern becomes immediately clear. The "1∅∅∅" established the beginning line number, and the "2∅∅" determined the spacing between lines.

Hit **BREAK** and type NEW again, then

```
AUTO 1∅∅∅
```

and

ENTER

a few times.

BREAK out of AUTO and start again with

```
AUTO 3∅∅∅∅,1
```

and a few **ENTER** s. Very handy with very big numbers. **BREAK**

How about

```
AUTO 17,4
```

You get the idea. It is even possible to use AUTO as a statement in a program, tho I can't think of any reasonable excuse for putting it there. Can you? Unless you specify otherwise, AUTO will always begin on line 1∅ and always space the lines 1∅ numbers apart.

One important caution. Whenever you get fooling with something that's automatic, a degree of personal control is lost. Enter this quickie:

    1Ø PRINT"NOW WHAT ARE WE UP TO?"

    2Ø PRINT"BEATS ME!"

    99 END

Then type

    AUTO

        . . . oh, oh! What does the

    1Ø*   mean?

The asterisk means that there is already a line number 1Ø, and if you hit **ENTER** it will erase the existing line 1Ø. That's fine if it's what you want. Otherwise, you MUST **BREAK** in order to escape.

The AUTO command is not just for the lazy, it can be a real time saver (and save mental energy as well). For the touch typist who doesn't have to look at the screen when typing fast, it's a real delight.

Part III

Advanced Concepts of
LEVEL II BASIC

"DAD SAID IT WOULD TAKE A LOT OF WORK TO CONVERT THESE LEVEL 1 TAPES TO LEVEL 11! SHUCKS, ALL I HAD TO DO WAS PENCIL IN ANOTHER 'I' ON THESE CASSETTE LABELS."

"OKAY! NOW ON TO THE NEXT CHAPTER!..."

CHAPTER 7

Converting Programs From

LEVEL I

to

LEVEL II

This chapter concentrates on converting existing Level I programs to Level II BASIC. Radio Shack furnishes a free set of tapes containing conversion programs for this purpose. Our task here is to learn how to use them to convert our old Level I tapes to Level II tapes.

If you are starting right out at Level II and have no Level I tapes to convert, you may skip this Chapter entirely, and proceed directly to the next one. You got plenty of practice changing the programs at the end of the Level I Manual to Level II.

Since we do not know the whole of Level II BASIC at this time, we are not going to make major program logic changes, only syntax changes. The idea is to make the programs RUN. In some cases, particularly where subroutines can be replaced with new intrinsic functions, you might wish to make such replacements. But, best you wait until we have studied them first . . .

Loading In The Program Conversion Tape

Since the conversion tape is to be loaded into a Level II machine, set up the recorder the same as for any other Level II tape. The volume control should be at about 5 (or wherever it works best).

Turn the Computer completely OFF using the POWER switch on the back; let it rest for a few seconds, then turn it back ON. It will then ask

MEMORY SIZE?_

If you have 16K of RAM you respond with

31477 **ENTER**

If you have 4K of RAM, type

19189 **ENTER**

The reason for engaging in this mysterious behavior is to temporarily set aside a number of memory cells to hold the special conversion program. It could be loaded in without this "set-aside", but if for some reason you have to type NEW (or need to convert a second Level I tape), the conversion program itself would be destroyed.

Now that memory space has been reserved for the conversion program, it takes some sleight of hand to get it loaded from the tape into the Computer. Following the usual READY and prompt, type

SYSTEM **ENTER**

The Computer will come back with

*?

after which you type

CONV **ENTER**

(CONV is the name of the conversion program.)

Look carefully at the PROGRAM CONVERSION TAPE. One side is for Computers with 16K of RAM, the other for those with 4K. Insert it in the recorder, correct side up (rewind it if necessary), and press the PLAY button. (Double-check to see that the volume is set at about 5.)

If you did everything right so far and the lights didn't dim, the tape should load into the Computer. (All this and we didn't even type CLOAD. Sort of makes you feel like you've lost control, doesn't it.)

It may take many seconds for the asterisks to start blinking in the upper right corner of the screen, but don't give up until the tape stops. If for some reason it doesn't "take", rewind the tape and try again. Try "tweaking" the volume control for the next try. If that doesn't work, clean the heads. Wiggle the cables. Move the power supply? Trade in the whole works for an IBM 370? Should there be trouble after several attempts, it's best to shut the Computer off and start the entire cycle over from the beginning. Once you get the hang of this, it goes pretty fast.

We'll assume the best — it loaded. Again the strange prompt returns, following which you must type some more heiro-glyphics: [/31478 (for 16K machines), or /1919Ø (for 4K machines)]

   *?/31478 **ENTER**

The Computer will come back and say:

   LOAD TAPE & PRESS ENTER

What it's really trying to say is:

"Take one of your old Level I tapes which contains a pro-gram you want to convert to Level II and put it in the record-er, just like you usually do. Be sure it is rewound, and set the volume control to about 8, or wherever you usually set it for loading Level I. Press the PLAY button on the recorder, then press **ENTER**."

The Level I tape should now load into your Level II machine, thinking it's a Level I. We've got the machine all faked out, and are safe as long as someone doesn't bump the power plug.

If it doesn't like the tape we feed it, the message

    LOAD TAPE & PRESS ENTER

is displayed again, and we try again, tweaking the volume control a bit.

If the Level I program was too long to fit in the remaining memory space (or the recording itself is a bit squirrely) the Computer says:

    PROGRAM TOO LONG

and returns to Level II BASIC with a READY.

This can happen even tho you might have used the same program on the same machine prior to upgrading it to Level II. Remember, we have about 15ØØ bytes of RAM set-aside to hold the CONVersion program, so there's not as much usable space as there was before.

If the program really *is* too long, there are several options:
1. If using a 4K machine, find a friend with a 16K version.
2. Take your bag of gold to the candy store for some more RAM.
3. If using a 16K machine, take your banker to the candy store for more RAM.
4. Write shorter programs.
5. Take up stamp collecting.

Assuming all went well however, the screen will read:

    PRESS ENTER   TO BEGIN

Now what that really means is: "Press the **ENTER** key to start the CONVersion program running." The CONVersion program is not a BASIC program, it's written in machine language. A bunch of ones and zero's talking gibberish to each other. That's why we didn't get to type RUN.

Press **ENTER** .

(If you listen very carefully you can hear the corn sheller running as the Level I program is being more or less converted to Level II.)

Now the screen says:

CONVERSION COMPLETE

PRESS ENTER TO CONTINUE

Go ahead, press **ENTER** , and the Computer responds with

READY

>_

Well — that's comforting. At least we know we are back in BASIC (Level II.) The program has been mostly converted, and we can finish the job by adding missing lines, editing out gliches and nonsense characters, and deleting such unnecessary things as trig subroutines. We have many more "intrinsic" functions in Level II and can scrap the special subroutines from Level I.

Sure, It Will Convert All Your Old Tapes (. . . well, almost)

If the program was very simple it may not need any editing, but chances are you will have to make some changes to complete the conversion. Here is a sample of things to look for:

1. Observe that all the old "shorthand" words (like P.) have been changed to "longhand". That means the program will require more memory to hold the longer words. In addition, if you have already used very long lines, tightly packed, they may now overflow and be too long. If so, extra lines can be added to take up the overflow.

2. The old PRINT AT graphic statements were changed to PRINT@. No problem here, but Level I was tolerant and allowed either a comma (,) or a semi-colon (;) after PRINT AT. Level II allows only the comma. Semi-colons will have to be changed.

113

3. Conversely, commas used after Level I PRINT TAB's have to be changed to semicolons or omitted entirely.

4. Level I did not require DIMensioning of arrays. Level II does, if they contain more than 11 elements ($\emptyset$-1$\emptyset$). A DIM statement will have to be added for each such array.

5. SET (127.47) cannot be exceeded in Level II. When they were exceeded in Level I they just started over again with zero. Edit or rewrite as necessary.

6. Level II executes programs faster than Level I. Numbers used for timing in FOR-NEXT loops will have to be changed.

7. Each subroutine should be examined to see if there is an intrinsic function available which does the same thing much faster and in less space.

8. Level II does not allow a variable to be input as a value for another variable. A little rewriting will take care of this one.

After The Ball Is Over

After all this falderall, the program conversion is complete. When the program RUNs to your satisfaction, you'll want to save it again on tape. Some users wish to have both Level I and II versions of their programs, leaving I on one side of a cassette recording and II on the flip side. Various coding schemes are helpful, such as colored stickers, "screw heads down" (the screws holding the tapes together) for Level I, "screw heads up" for Level II, etc. If *you* don't care to keep Level I programs around, the above is all just academic.

Anyhoo . . . we do want to save the Level II version. Set up the recorder as usual. CSAVE "A" the program on cassette several times, for safety. CLOAD? the tape (with the volume control back at 5) as a double-check. If all is well, mission accomplished.

TO CONVERT THE NEXT TAPED PROGRAM

If you didn't shut off the Computer, the CONVersion program is still in there. So is the converted BASIC program. Type NEW to sweep out the BASIC program. The CONversion program is safe in the protected area set-aside.

To prepare the Computer to accept the next Level I tape for conversion we again type:

SYSTEM **ENTER**

*?/31478 **ENTER**

(or /1919Ø **ENTER** if 4K RAM)

and follow the instructions on the screen as before. Be sure to adjust the volume to match the tape being played.

CONVERTING DATA STORAGE TAPES

Level I had a limited Cassette DATA File capability. Cassette DATA tapes are accessed by *programs*, which are on another tape and also have to be converted. See Appendix B of the Level I User's Manual for more information. (Extra copies of the Manual are available through all Radio Shack stores as Catalog #62-2016 at the token price of $5.95.)

There is serious question whether the hassle of converting DATA tapes is worth the effort. If you have the DATA written down somewhere it may be easier to re-enter it via the keyboard using your Level I control program converted to Level II. If you don't have the DATA written down, write a short program in Level I which will read the DATA off tape and present it on the screen or printer for copying. For those readers who are brutes for punishment, we'll go through the DATA tape conversion procedure anyway.

Using the procedures discussed in the first section, convert your Control Program tape to Level II. Test it on some dummy DATA to make sure it's sound.

Prepare the Computer to accept the Level I DATA tapes by typing

    SYSTEM

        which calls up

    *?

        and we answer with DCONV

DCONV is the name of the DataCONVersion program. Both sides of this tape are the same so we needn't worry about computer memory size. The recorder should be set to about 5. Pop in the tape, press the PLAY key, and watch the asterisks.

When the prompt returns

    *?

        type /17152

The Computer will say

    TO READ IN DATA

    LOAD THE LEVEL-I TAPE & PRESS ENTER _

This means, insert your old Level I DATA tape in the recorder. Change the volume control to about 8 and press the PLAY key; then press **ENTER**.

After the first short block of DATA has been loaded into the Computer (watch the asterisks and listen for the clicking relay), the screen will direct:

    TO RECORD DATA,

    LOAD THE LEVEL-II TAPE & PRESS ENTER_

Freely translated, this says you should remove the Level I tape now in the recorder, being careful not to let the tape move. Put a fresh tape in the recorder and set it up to record. Then – press **ENTER**

Following a brief recording interlude, the screen will clear and say

IF YOU HAVE MORE DATA ON THE LEVEL-I TAPE,

RELOAD IT (DO NOT REWIND) AND TYPE 1,

ELSE TYPE 2_

Translation: "You have now converted one short block of DATA from Level I to Level II. Would you care to try again? If so, carefully remove the Level II tape now in the recorder, marking the cassette so you don't get it all mixed up with the others. Insert the old original Level I DATA tape back into the recorder, press the PLAY button, then type the number 1. If on the other hand you don't have any more DATA to convert (or are just going to chuck this whole complicated business), type 2 and go fishing."

Assuming you optioned to convert some more DATA and typed 1, the same thing happened as before. A short block of DATA was fed into the Computer, was converted to Level II, and the screen again directs:

TO RECORD DATA,

LOAD THE LEVEL-II TAPE & PRESS ENTER_

On and on it goes . . .

Be sure that throughout this process you keep a careful count of how many pieces of DATA you have to convert, and a running count as they are converted. If you lose count, you may have to start all over again — not a pleasant thought.

When done converting DATA tapes, return the Computer back to its normal Level II BASIC mode by typing

2

once or twice. Failing that, turn it off, then on again.

Load in the converted PROGRAM tape and try it out with the converted DATA tape. If it all works, you're back in business — at Level II.

CHAPTER 8
The ASCII Set

The purpose of this chapter is to learn how to use ASC and CHR$. Before doing so however, we must learn about something called "the ASCII set". ASCII is pronounced (ASK'-EE) and it stands for American Standard Code for Information Interchange. Since a computer stores and processes only numbers, not letters or punctuation, it's important that there be some sort of uniform system to specify which numbers represent which letters and symbols. The ASCII Chart in Appendix B shows the relationship between the number system and symbols as used in your Level II TRS-80.

Type this program into your Computer:

```
1Ø  FOR N = Ø TO 255

2Ø  PRINT "ASCII NUMBER";N;

3Ø  PRINT "STANDS FOR",CHR$(N)

4Ø  FOR T = 1 TO 5ØØ : NEXT T

5Ø  NEXT N
```

As you RUN it, observe that the characters beteen ASCII code numbers 32 and 126 are printed on the screen. Those numbers from 97 to 122 are just lower-case duplicates of numbers 65 to 90, but the TRS-80 prints only upper case. The other code numbers in that range stand for capabilities which do not print on the screen.

In case you end up in the Big House serving time for computer fraud, this little program will make up your license plate combinations, putting CHR$ to good use. Pay special attention to line 4∅. With the aid of the ASCII chart in Appendix B, can you see why CHR$(RND(26)+64) creates letters? Think it through, then type:

```
1 CLS

1∅ REM * LICENSE PLATE NUMBER GENERATOR *

2∅ FOR N=1 TO 3 : PRINT RND(1∅)-1;

3∅ NEXT N : PRINT " ";

4∅ FOR N=1 TO 3 : PRINT CHR$(RND(26)+64);

5∅ PRINT " "; : NEXT N : PRINT, : GOTO 2∅
```

and RUN

Did you think it through?

The RND generator in line 4∅ spits out numbers between 1 and 26. We add 64 to each number to make the sum fall in the range between 65 and 9∅. What do we see on the ASCII conversion chart between 65 and 9∅. Hmmmm???

The ASCII code numbers between Ø and 31 are used for special control requirements in the TRS-80:

Code	Function
0-7	None
8	Backspaces and erases current character
9	None
1Ø-13	Carriage returns
14	Turns on cursor
15	Turns off cursor
16-22	None
23	Converts to 32 character mode
24	Backspace ← Cursor
25	Advance → Cursor
26	Downward ↓ linefeed
27	Upward ↑ linefeed
28	Home, return cursor to display position(Ø,Ø)
29	Move cursor to beginning of line
3Ø	Erases to the end of the line
31	Clear to the end of the frame

The Code numbers between 128 and 191 are for graphics characters, nearly all of which are irrelevant for the ordinary computer user. SET, RESET and POINT serve most everyday needs.

The ASCII numbers between 192 and 255 are so called "space compression codes". You can use them to insert from Ø to 63 blank spaces in a printed line. Code 192 stands for Ø spaces and 255 stands for 63 spaces. The in-between numbers correspond accordingly. Erase the memory and RUN this program:

```
1Ø PRINT"HELLO OUT";CHR$(222);"THERE"
```

As you can see, CHR$(222) inserted 3Ø blanks, or "tabbed over" 3Ø spaces between OUT and THERE. To see the difference between using these ASCII code numbers and using TAB, add this line:

```
2Ø PRINT"HELLO OUT";TAB(3Ø);"THERE"
```

and RUN.

TAB spaces from the **beginning** of the line, while this series of ASCII numbers actually inserts spaces from the **last** PRINT position in the line.

There is in practice little uniformity internationally (or even inside the U.S.) in the use of ASCII code numbers other than those used for just letters and numbers. Fortunately, that is sufficient for most of our everyday needs. If you contemplate the problems faced by the Japanese, Arabs and others who need special letters and characters, you will get some idea of how these numbers between 127 and 255 can be put to good use.

So What is CHR$(N)??

We have used CHR$ freely so far without describing it, but you've undoubtedly figured it out anyway. CHR$(N) produces the ASCII character (or control action) specified by the code **number** N. It is a one-way converter from the ASCII **code** to the ASCII **character**, and allows us to throw characters around with the ease of throwing around numbers.

Enter this simple program:

```
1Ø INPUT "TYPE ANY NUMBER BETWEEN 33 AND 127";N

2Ø PRINT CHR$(N)

3Ø RUN
```

and RUN

Almost all of our activity with ASCII numbers will be confined to this range. However, these "quickie" programs show how to use several ASCII numbers that stand for **actions** instead of numbers, letters or characters. Give them a try:

```
1Ø REM   * CURSOR BLINKER *

2Ø PRINT CHR$(14);

3Ø FOR N=1 TO 5ØØ : NEXT N

4Ø PRINT CHR$(15);

5Ø FOR N=1 TO 5ØØ : NEXT N

6Ø GOTO 2Ø
```

And

```
1 REM   * DOUBLE WIDTH DEMO *

1Ø CLS

2Ø PRINT CHR$(23)

3Ø PRINT@462,"HELLO OUT THERE"

4Ø FOR X=1 TO 5ØØ : NEXT X

5Ø PRINT CHR$(28)

6Ø FOR X=1 TO 5ØØ : NEXT X

7Ø GOTO 2Ø
```

123

The use of double width letters adds considerable impact to visual displays. There are however several rules which must be followed. Type in this program, then we'll explore them:

```
10 REM  * ON BASE OF STATUE OF LIBERTY *
20 REM  * LARGEST STATUE EVER ERECTED *
30 CLS : PRINT CHR$(23)
40 PRINT@456, "KEEP,  ANCIENT LANDS, "
50 PRINT@522, "YOUR STORIED POMP!"
60 FOR T=1TO1700 : NEXT
70 CLS : PRINT CHR$(23)
80 PRINT@128, "GIVE ME YOUR TIRED, YOUR POOR, "
90 FOR T = 1 TO 1500 : NEXT
100 PRINT@256, "YOUR HUDDLED MASSES YEARNING TO"
110 PRINT@324, "BREATHE FREE, "
120 FOR T = 1 TO 1100 : NEXT
130 PRINT@448, "THE WRETCHED REFUSE OF YOUR"
140 PRINT@516, "TEEMING SHORE. "
150 FOR T = 1 TO 1900 : NEXT
160 PRINT@640, "SEND THESE,  THE HOMELESS, "
170 PRINT@708, "TEMPEST-TOST TO ME, "
180 FOR T = 1 TO 2000 : NEXT
190 PRINT@832, "I LIFT MY LAMP BESIDE THE GOLDEN"
200 PRINT@900, "DOOR!"
210 GOTO210
```

and RUN.

In line 30 we used ASCII character 23 to convert the video display to 32 characters per line. In line 70 we needed a CLS, but CLS automatically returns the video to 64 characters per line. This forced us to use another CHR$(23) to get back in the 32 character mode.

Look at each PRINT@ statement. See anything at all similar ... something we haven't discussed? How about it, Sherlock? (Shut up Watson! We know you see it.) Elementary, when you stop and think about it. Every video starting address ends in an even number. *Oh, yes ... (cough) ... of course.*

Every letter and number is printed double-width, and the rules state that for double width we must start on an even numbered block. Change line 4Ø to PRINT@457 instead of 456 and RUN.

Total wipeout! Can't get much more dramatic than that. Add 1 more number to make it PRINT@458

and RUN.

Notice anything? Look at the display very carefully. Then change the program line back to PRINT@456

and RUN.

See it?

Right! We have to move over 2 video print addresses to move the double-width display over just 1 space. Terribly obvious when you think of it. Not very obvious when trying to trouble-shoot a program and you aren't aware of it.

This program needs a good graphics display of The Statue, complete with flaming torch. Also, a good paper printout to hang on the wall. How about it, artists?

What then is ASC($)?

ASC is the exact opposite of CHR$(N). ASC is a one-way converter from the ASCII character to its corresponding ASCII **number**.

Type:

```
1Ø INPUT "TYPE ALMOST ANY LETTER, NUMBER
                OR CHARACTER":A$

2Ø PRINT"ITS ASCII NUMBER IS";ASC(A$)

3Ø PRINT

4Ø GOTO 1Ø
```

and RUN.

It will print the ASCII number of almost all characters. (I don't have any idea why this particular computer doesn't work with , " : and some others, but then strings can be a real mystery at times as we will see in the next chapters.)

The second way to use ASC is to imbed the character within quotes, thus:

```
10 PRINT ASC("A")
```

This latter method always seems to work with this particular interpreter, but isn't always convenient.

Before we can really understand what we are doing, we must learn a lot more about strings. Before we could learn about strings we had to learn something about ASCII. It's like "catch TRS-80".

On to the next Chapter.

NOTES

Strings in General

It was not our intention to "string you along" in the previous Chapter, but we can't really understand how strings work without first understanding the ASCII concept of numbers standing for letters, numbers and other characters and control functions.

Level I BASIC allowed for only 2 strings — A$ and B$ — and they were not very powerful. We could INPUT a name or READ a string from DATA and use the STRINGs in PRINT statements, but that was about all. You'll be glad to know that Level II BASIC has every string capability usually associated with BASIC.

Comparing Strings

Among the most powerful string handling capability we need is the ability to compare them. We compare numbers in NUMERIC variables all the time. How can we compare strings of letters or words? Well, why do you suppose we put the ASCII Chapter just before this one? *Right!* The Computer can compare the ASCII **code numbers** of letters and other characters. The effective result is a comparison of what's in the corresponding strings.

Type in this program:

```
1 CLS
1Ø INPUT"WHAT IS YOUR NAME";A$
2Ø IF A$ = "ISHKIBIBBLE" THEN 5Ø
3Ø PRINT"SORRY. YOUR NAME ISN'T ISHKIBIBBLE
                            - SO GET LOST!"
4Ø END
5Ø PRINT"IT'S ABOUT TIME. FORGET HOW
                  TO SPELL YOUR NAME?"
```

and RUN.

If the Computer can compare **that** name it should be able to compare anything!

During the process of comparing what you enter as A$ in line
1Ø to what's already in quotes in line 2Ø, the ASCII code
numbers of each letter found in one string are compared,
letter for letter, from left to right with those in the other.
Every one must match, or the test fails.

String and "quotes" go together like beer and chocolate
cake. *(Beer and chocolate cake ...?)* You know
this from Level I where every PRINT "XXX" has its string
enclosed in quotes ... or it won't work (PRINT "XXX" is
called a string **constant**, compared with A$, a string **variable**.)
RUN the above program again, this time answering the question with "ISHKIBBLE", but enclosed in quotes.

Sure — it ran OK. Worked either with or without quotes.
Interpreters have become increasingly lenient about this
matter, but every once in a while the rules come up from
behind and bite you if you play fast and loose with them.

If you INPUT a string, and it has no commas, semicolons,
leading or trailing spaces in it, you don't need to enclose it in
quotes. You will never go wrong by ALWAYS enclosing
strings in quotes, but that can be a nuisance.

Erase the resident program and type in this next one, which
READs string data from a DATA line.

```
1 CLS

1Ø READ A$,B$,C$

2Ø PRINT A$

3Ø PRINT B$

4Ø PRINT C$

1ØØ DATA COMPUSOFT PUBLISHING, SAN DIEGO, CA, 92119
```

and RUN

Look carefully at the results. The screen shows:

```
COMPUTSOFT PUBLISHING

SAN DIEGO

CA
```

That's fine, but where is the ZIP CODE??? And why didn't SAN DIEGO and CA get printed on the same line? The answer, my friend, is blowing in the . . . er, in the commas. Ahem.

Because of the commas in the DATA line, the READ statement sees 4 pieces of DATA, but only READs 3 of them. What do we have to do in order to PRINT a comma as part of a string? Right — enclose it, or the string containing it, in quotes.

```
EDIT1ØØ
```

and change line 1ØØ to read

```
1ØØ DATA COMPUSOFT PUBLISHING, "SAN DIEGO, CA", 92119
```

and RUN.

Aaaah! That's more like it. Notice that we didn't have to enclose all pieces of string DATA in separate quotes, but we could have.

What would happen if we enclosed the **entire** DATA line in quotes, leaving the existing quotes in there? (Think about it, but don't neglect to try it. Every question raised has a specific purpose.)

Our editor is so easy to use, let's:

```
1ØØ DATA"COMPUSOFT PUBLISHING,"SAN DIEGO, CA", 92119"
```

and RUN.

Awwk! Disaster . . . A syntax error? Yes, there is no straight forward way to print quotes as part of a string constant, even by enclosing them inside another pair of quotes. The Computer just isn't smart enough to figure out which quote mark is which. The usual way to overcome this standard deficiency is to substitute ' for '', inside other quotes. Let's try it.

```
100 DATA"COMPUSOFT PUBLISHING,'SAN DIEGO, CA', 92119"
```

and RUN.

Ooops, ?OD (OUT OF DATA) error in 10? Of course. With quotes surrounding the whole works there is now just one piece of DATA and we are trying to read 3 pieces. Let's change line 10 to just read one piece:

```
10 READ A$
```

and RUN again.

There we go. Might look a little strange, but it proves the point and warns us a little about the "touchiness" of strings.

When it comes to strings, that classic old ballad from the hills is so appropriate:

"Ah-cigareets, and whuisky, and wild computers, they'll drive you crazy, they'll drive you insane!"

But, undaunted by this high class philosophy, we launch our vessel towards the next chapter.

As the sun sinks slowly in the west, tropical breezes fill our sails and water laps against the bow. Stars appear, and from the beach fires plaintive native chants are heard, calling . . .

" OF WHUISKY AND WILD COMPUTERS.."

..." I WISH HE WAS ON THE RADIO... ...THEN WE COULD TURN HIM OFF.."

NOTES

LEN, DEFSTR,

CLEAR and DIM

One of the most frequently needed pieces of information about a string is its length. Fortunately, the LEN function makes it easy to find. Type:

```
1 CLS : PRINT

1Ø INPUT"ENTER A STRING OF CHARACTERS";A$

2Ø L = LEN(A$)

3Ø PRINT A$;" HAS";L;"CHARACTERS"

9Ø PRINT : LIST
```

RUN several times entering your name and other combinations of letters and numbers. Try entering your name, last name first, with a comma after your last name.

AHA! Can't input a comma. How about if we put it all in quotes? Try again.

Yep. Just like it said in the last Chapter.

LEN has only one significant variation, and it's not all that useful — unless you really need it. Change lines 1Ø-3Ø to read:

```
1Ø INPUT "ENTER A NUMBER";A

2Ø L = LEN(A)

3Ø PRINT A;" HAS";L;"CHARACTERS"
```

and RUN.

Crash time again! TM ERROR means we tried to input a number into LEN — but it requires a string input. OK, let's change LEN to make it a string:

```
2Ø L = LEN("A")
```

and RUN, entering a number.

Hmmm. Doesn't seem to matter what number we enter, it always comes back saying that we have only 1 character.

The answer is, LEN evaluates the length of what is actually between its parentheses (or quotes). At first we brought in a string from the "outside" and measured its length. That worked fine. We are now measuring the length of what's between the quotes, and that **length** doesn't change with the **value** of A.

Like we said, this second way to use LEN has its limitations, but does tell us the length of what's there. (Change the resident program back to the way it appears at the beginning of the Chapter.)

DEFSTR — For Thrill Seekers Only

Those among us who attract trouble will love this next one. As if handling strings isn't complex enough, this very powerful Statement looks nice and clean but can be the greatest source of heartburn since the horseradish pizza.

DEFSTR allows us to define which variables are to be string variables, so we don't have to use $ any more. *(Hmm . . . Uncle Sam could put some of this DEFSTR business to good use.)* Add this line:

```
5 DEFSTR A
```

and use the Editor to remove the $ in lines 1Ø, 2Ø, and 3Ø. Then RUN.

Works great, doesn't it. A was declared by line 5 to be a string variable. So what's all the fuss about?

Well, this is a very simple program, but let's change 5 to read:

```
5 DEFSTR A-Z
```

which makes **all** letters string variables

and RUN.

Crasho again! The L in line 2∅ is now **also** a string. Since LEN gives us a number as the length of a string, it doesn't set at all well with L (really L string). Imagine the fun this can create in a long program.

DEFSTR follows the same format as the other DEF functions, with DEFSTR A,B,C also being a legal statement.

It Came Upon a Midnight CLEAR
(Is that like a midnight requisition?)

When the Computer is first turned on, 5∅ bytes of memory space are set aside for use by strings — **all** strings combined. Not very much space if we're into a biggie. At the command level, type NEW, then:

```
>PRINT FRE(A$)
```

It asks the Computer "how much space is left for strings?". Not only A$, but **all** strings. The "A$" is just a "dummy" we have to use with FRE. B$, C$, or anything similar would work just as well. (PRINT FRE(X) with most characters but without the $ sign tells us the same thing as MEM — how much **total** memory space is available.)

The Computer should respond with

5Ø

The CLEAR command/statement allows us to change the amount of reserved string space to anything we want, up to almost the total available memory. Going the other way, we can eliminate all reserved space, leaving all memory for non-string use. Let's play around with some combinations and see what happens:

>CLEAR Ø

>PRINT FRE(A$)

>Ø

Is that what you got? CLEARed zero and got zero? Good.

Type NEW and measure again.

>NEW

>PRINT FRE(A$)

>Ø

What? Still zero? That's right. The CLEAR command is a high level one and is not affected by NEW. "Power-up" automatically sets aside 5Ø bytes, and wherever we reset it, there it stays until it's reset again.

Try:

>PRINT MEM

>15565

> (I've got the keyboard debounce loaded in. You might get a little different number — but it should be in the ballpark.)

138

```
>CLEAR MEM/4

>PRINT FRE(A$)

>398Ø
```

We just arbitrarily said, "Let's set aside a fourth of the memory for use by strings." CLEAR MEM/4 did it. If it turns out to be too much (wasteful) or too little (Computer will say ?OS) it's easily changed. A very adept programmer could even come up with an error-trapping routine that would CLEAR additional memory as needed if an ?OS message came through, and the operator wouldn't even know that something happened.

PRINT FRE(X$) can also be used as a program statement. Try it in any program using strings to watch what happens.

Type:

```
>CLEAR 5Ø
```

and get us back to "normal."

New DIMensions

DIM is to arrays what CLEAR is to strings. We already did some DIMensioning in the Level I book with single dimension **numeric** arrays. When we have a string array we have to do the same thing.

Suppose we have a program like this: (Type it in)

```
1 CLS : PRINT

1Ø FOR N = 1 TO 16

2Ø READ A$(N)

3Ø PRINT A$(N),

4Ø NEXT N

9Ø PRINT : LIST

1ØØ DATA ALPHA, BRAVO, CHARLIE, DELTA,
                           ECHO, FOXTROT

11Ø DATA GOLF, HOTEL, INDIA, JAPAN,
                      KILO, LIMA, MIKE

12Ø DATA NOVEMBER, OSCAR, PAPA
```

       and RUN.

Oops. There's a problem. ?BS ERROR means "not enough space set aside for an array." You'll recall that only 11 elements **per array** (from Ø-1Ø) are set aside on power-up. We are trying to read in 16 of them, starting with 1. The solution:

```
>5 DIM A$(16)
```

       and RUN.

That's better. DIMensioning a string array is just like dimensioning a numeric one — just call it by its name. In this case, its name is A$. You "high speed" types will want to know that to do "dynamic redimensioning" (that's doing it while the program is running), the program must encounter a CLEAR first. Oh.

CONCATENATION

Concatenation? Concatenation??? Now what is that supposed to mean? Isn't even in the dictionary. Did you ever wonder who pays who to sit around and think up such non-descriptive words? Must have been done on a government grant. Wait till Senator Proxmire hears about it.

Concatenation (pronounced con-cat-uh-na'tion) is a national debt-sized word which means "add". In our case it means "add strings together". It's easier to do than to pronounce.

Let's change our resident program a bit to make it read:

```
1 CLS : PRINT

1Ø FOR N = 1 TO 16

2Ø READ A$

25 B$ = B$ + A$

3Ø PRINT B$

4Ø NEXT N

9Ø PRINT : LIST

1ØØ DATA ALPHA, BRAVO, CHARLIE, DELTA,
          ECHO, FOXTROT, GOLF, HOTEL

11Ø DATA INDIA, JAPAN, KILO, LIMA,
          MIKE, NOVEMBER, OSCAR, PAPA
```

Check it carefully but don't RUN it yet. The key line is 25, which simply says B$ (a new variable) equals the old B$ (which starts out as nothing) plus whatever is in A$. It then cycles around and keeps adding what is in B$ to what is READ from DATA as A$. Now RUN.

Gotcha! We ran out of string space, says the ?OS. B$ just keeps growing and growing until the 5Ø byte set-aside isn't enough.

How much is enough? Easy question, tough answer. The VARPTR statement will give us the answer, but its use requires a PhD from the funny farm where they only talk in ones and zeros.

The easiest way is to stay within the noblest engineering tradition — add some more string space and see what happens. It's "cut and try" time.

```
5 CLEAR 1ØØ
```

      and

```
RUN
```

Getting closer. Let's try again. (This warms the cockles of any true experimenter's heart — and drives any true theoretical scientist right up the wall. Chuckle.)

```
5 CLEAR 15Ø
```

```
RUN
```

Still not enough. Looks close though, doesn't it?

```
5 CLEAR 175
```

```
RUN
```

Sweet success. All due to our extensive planning, no doubt.

Better do a quick

>PRINT MEM

to see that there's plenty of space left — and there is.

The purist will keep experimenting and find out that we need exactly . . . (. . *message garbled in transmission* . .) . . . bytes of string space to make the program RUN, yet not waste any. (Hint: If you add the number of characters in the last line printed to those in the next-to-last line, you'll be so close to the answer it may bite you. We could even figure that one out in advance.)

Anyhoo, the point of all this is concatenation. Line 25 just did it, and that's about all there is to it. We added strings together.

Not done playing you say? OK, you non-believers, have some fun with this simple program:

```
1 CLEAR 35

1Ø REM * CLEAR DEMO *

2Ø A$="Ø" : B$="/"

3Ø PRINT A$;LEN(A$)

4Ø A$ = A$ + B$

5Ø GOTO 3Ø
```

In the next chapter we learn how to tear strings into little pieces. We've just learned how to put them back together. (Somebody got something backwards here . . .)

"IF THAT MACHINE OF YOURS IS SO GREAT
LET'S SEE IT SEARCH THROUGH THIS
CLEAN LAUNDRY AND SORT OUT
YOUR SOCKS!"

HOW DO YOU WRITE A
SUB ROUTINE TO LOOK
UNDER THE BED?

Rich Barnes

CHAPTER 11

Search and Sort

One of the Computer's most powerful features is its ability to search through a pile of DATA and SORT the findings into some order. Alphabetical, reverse alphabetical, numerical from smallest to largest, or the reverse — all are common. This feature is so important we are going to spend this entire chapter learning how to use it.

Typical applications of search and sort include:

1. Arranging a list of customers' or prospects' names in alphabetical order.

2. Sorting names in zip-code order for lower-cost mailing.

3. Sorting the names of clients in phone area code order.

While not really all that complicated, the sorting process is sufficiently rigorous that we are going to take it *very slowly* and examine each step. Once we get the hang of it, the Computer can blaze away without our considering the staggering number of steps it's going through.

Let's start with a problem. We have the names of 8 customers (if that doesn't grab you, make it 8 million — the process is identical). We need to arrange them in alphabetical order.

We start by storing their names in a DATA line. Type in:

```
1ØØØ DATA BRAVO, XRAY, ALPHA, ZEBRA,
     FOXTROT, TANGO, HOTEL, SIERRA
```

Since we are sorting by name rather than by number, we have to use string variables, string arrays, etc. They work equally well with numbers such as zip codes, while numeric variables and arrays work **only** with numbers.

The backbone of a sort routine is the array. Each name has to be READ from DATA into an array. So:

```
1Ø REM * ALPHA SORT OF STRINGS FROM DATA *

2Ø CLS : FOR D = 1 TO 8 : READ A$(D) :
                    N=N+1 : NEXT D
```

Line 1Ø is of course just the title

Line 2Ø clears the screen, then "loads the array" by READing the 8 names into storage slots A$(1) to A$(8). N is simply a counter which will follow through the rest of the program. In this simple program we could have made N=8, since we know how many names we have. In the next sample program we won't know how many names there are, so let's leave N the way it's usually used.

Important to the sort routine are 2 nested FOR-NEXT loops.

1. The first one, F, controls the First name.

2. S, the second one, controls the name to be compared against the first one.

   Names and words are compared as we learned in the section on ASCII, *remember?*

Let's establish our loops first, then fill in the guts later:

```
3Ø FOR F = 1 TO N-1 'F=FIRST WORD TO
                         BE COMPARED

4Ø  FOR S = F+1 TO N 'S=SECOND WORD TO
                          BE COMPARED

9Ø  NEXT S           ' MAKES 7 PASSES

1ØØ NEXT F           ' MAKES 7 PASSES
```

It may seem puzzling that F and S only have to make 7
passes when there are 8 names. Think of it this way. Whatever word isn't smaller (ASCII #) than the rest, just ends up
last. No need to test again to prove that.

The F loop READs array elements 1 through 7 (N−1 = 7).
The S loop READs array elements 2 through 8. This always
provides us with **different** array elements to compare against
each other.

Now let's jump to the end of our program and prepare it to
PRINT out what we are about to do. Type:

```
11Ø FOR D = 1 TO N : PRINT A$(D), : NEXT D
```

When the sorting is done, the contents of A$(1) to A$(8)
will be the same as read from DATA, but will be in alphabetical order. We'll PRINT the array contents on the screen.

Now for the sort routine itself. Type:

```
5Ø    IF A$(F) <= A$(S) THEN 9Ø   'TEST
                        FOR SMALLER ASCII#

6Ø    T$ = A$(F)         ' TEMPORARY STORAGE
                           FOR FIRST WORD

7Ø  A$(F) = A$(S)        ' COPY SECOND WORD
                           TO FIRST PLACE

8Ø  A$(S) = T$           ' SWITCH FIRST WORD
                           TO SECOND PLACE
```

And there is the biggie! If you can follow those 4 lines the rest is duck soup.

> Line 5Ø says "if the first word is smaller than (or equal to) to the second word, leave well enough alone and bail out of this routine by going to line 9Ø, which will end this pass and READ another word to compare against F. If not, drop to the next line."

> Line 6Ø says, "Oh, they weren't in the right order, eh? We'll just store the First word in a temporary storage location called T$ and hold it there for future use. I'm sure we'll need it again."

> Line 7Ø copies the name held in the second cell into the first array cell. If the second one had an earlier starting letter than the first one, we do want to do this, don't we?

> Line 8Ø completes the switch by copying the name temporarily held in T$ into the second array cell. A$(1) and A$(2) contents have now been exchanged with the aid of the temporary holding pen, T$.

Us simple country boys find this one easy. There are two brahma bulls in separate pens, A$(1) & A$(2), and we want to switch them around. Ain't no way we're going to put them in the same pen at the same time. (Not with me in there anyway. Already broken too many 2 by 4's between their horns, and have some scars in the wrong end from escapes that were a hair too slow.) That's why we keep a temporary holding pen called T$. Got it?

If we did everything right, the program should:

> RUN.

and in a flash the names appear on the screen in alphabetical order:

ALPHA	BRAVO	FOXTROT
		HOTEL
SIERRA	TANGO	XRAY
		ZEBRA

Printing will be in standard 16 space tab zone format (sorry we can't put it all on one line in the book).

RUN it to your heart's delight. It's one of the most powerful things your Computer can do, and does it so well. Exactly the same thing takes place with a very long list of names (or zip codes, or whatever) but we would of course have to reDIMension for a larger array and CLEAR more string space.

Aw c'mon Horse — Whoa!

To get a really good look at what's happening, it's necessary to slow the beast **way** down, and insert a few extra PRINT lines. This lets us examine what's going on inside by watching the tube.

Add these temporaries:

```
45        PRINT F;A$(F),,S;A$(S)

47        FOR Z = 1 TO 1ØØØ : NEXT Z

55        PRINT "              <<--<<
                    SWITCHEROO"

85        PRINT F;A$(F),,S;A$(S)
```

(Allow four spaces after the arrow — that way it will look nice on the screen when you run it.)

    and RUN.

If that isn't slow enough, change line 47 so there is time for you to completely think it through. Pretend you're the Computer and make the decision that line 5Ø has to make. Take it from the top — very slowly! RUN.

1 BRAVO   2 XRAY

Means "in cell #1 is the word BRAVO. In cell #2 is the word XRAY". (Just like they came from the DATA line.) Of those two words, BRAVO is the "smallest" (ASCII#), so let's leave it in number 1 place. Onto the next pass of S.

1 BRAVO   3 ALPHA

Oops. BRAVO is in #1 and ALPHA is in #3, but ALPHA is smaller than BRAVO. We better switch them around. So

              <<--<<   SWITCHEROO

1 ALPHA   3 BRAVO

Don't worry too much about what is happening in the second column. S is scanning through the array and its contents are always changing, testing against what's in the first column. It's what **ends up** in the first column that counts — and it should be in increasing alphabetical order.

As the program keeps RUNning, watch the new words appear in S, the second loop and column, and compare them against what's in F, the first one. Try to guess what the Computer's going to do. Also keep an eye on the increasing numbers on the left. It's the **final word** with a given number in the first column that which will appear in the final printout.

RUN the program as many times as it takes (and at as many sessions as it takes) to really follow what's happening. It's awfully clever, and awfully important. We can carry this principle over to many useful programs in the future, but only if we *really* understand it.

When you feel it's under control, let's add one more little display to the screen. What is T$ holding while all this sorting is going on? Add to these lines so they read:

```
45 PRINT F;A$(F),,A;A$(S),"T$=";T$

85 PRINT F;A$(F),,S;A$(S),"T$=";T$
```

     and RUN.

"T$=" starts off with nothing since there is nothing in the holding pen. As F gets replaced in the switching process, however, T$ holds it. On a clear head it's not hard to follow what's happening. You'll probably want to save this program on tape and review it several times for a deep understanding of the process.

Sorting from the Outside

We don't really have to keep all our names, numbers or other information in DATA lines. It can be INPUT from the keyboard, from cassette tape, or from disk. The following program is quite similar to the first, and the logic is identical. Change these resident program lines:

```
5 D=1 : REM * ALPHA SORT OF NAMES VIA
                            INPUT *

1Ø INPUT"NEXT NAME";A$(D)  :  IF A$(D)="END"
                          GOTO 3Ø

2Ø D=D+1 : N=N+1 : GOTO 1Ø
```

Delete line 1ØØØ

and RUN.

Enter several random names, and when finished, enter the word "END". The process displayed on the screen will be identical to what we saw before.

Can you see the potential for all this?

CHAPTER 12

VAL($)
and
STR$(N)

The "hassle factor" is unusually high when converting back and forth between strings and numerics.

By definition, if we convert a numeric variable (can hold only a number) to a string variable (can hold most anything), the **content** of that string is still the number. No letters or other characters were converted since they weren't in the numeric variable to start with.

Conversely, if we change a string variable to a numeric variable, we can't change any letters or other characters to numbers. Only the numbers in a string can be converted to a numeric variable. (Don't get this confused with ASCII conversions.)

If you'll keep the 2 previous paragraphs in mind, it'll save an awful lot of grief in dealing with strings.

VAL

Let's give string-to-numeric conversion a shot. The VAL function converts a STRING variable holding a **number** into a **number**. Enter this VAL program:

```
1 CLS : PRINT

1Ø INPUT"WHAT STRING SHOULD I CONVERT TO
                            A NUMBER";A$

2Ø A = VAL(A$)

3Ø PRINT"THE NUMERIC VALUE OF ";A$;" IS";A

9Ø PRINT : LIST
```

and RUN.

Try lots of different inputs, such as:

```
12345

ASDF

123ASD

ASD123

1,2,3

A,B,C
```

and the same ones over again, but enclosed in quotes.

The tube tells all.

Using the Editor, take the $ out of lines 1Ø, 2Ø and 3Ø and RUN, INPUTting both numbers and letters, and RUN.

What you're seeing is typical of the frustrations that bedevil string users who don't follow the rules. VAL only evaluates **STRINGs**, and we've put A, a numeric value, in where a string belongs.

Let's put that A in quotes and see what happens.

```
2Ø A = VAL("A")
```

    and RUN.

No help at all! The rule remains unchanged. VAL converts a STRING holding a **number** into that **number**. Looking at the screen, we see it's just not in the cards. Remember this frustration when you get in the thick of debugging a nasty string-loaded program.

STR$

Now let's try the opposite, converting a numeric variable to a string variable. Change the program to read:

```
1 CLS : PRINT

1Ø INPUT"WHAT NUMERIC SHOULD I CONVERT
                    TO A STRING";A

2Ø A$ = STR$(A)

3Ø PRINT"THE STRING VALUE OF";A;"IS";A$

9Ø PRINT : LIST
```

    and RUN, using the same INPUTs we used when wringing out LEN.

There you have it. A short but very important Chapter. You should spend as much time on this one as any other chapter. If you really learn the pitfalls in using these 2 powerful functions, the returns will come back manyfold in debugging time.

Having a Ball

With

STRING

Three different but very similar functions are used for playing powerful games with strings. They are LEFT$, RIGHT$ and MID$. Let's start our exercise of them with this program:

```
1 CLS : PRINT

3Ø S$ = "KILROY WAS HERE"

6Ø PRINT LEFT$(S$,6),

7Ø PRINT MID$(S$,8,3),

8Ø PRINT RIGHT$(S$,4)

9Ø PRINT : LIST
```

and RUN.

The screen shows:

```
KILROY          WAS             HERE
```

(How about that one, nostalgia buffs?)

Learning to use these functions is exceedingly simple. Study the program slowly and carefully as we explain what happened.

LEFT$ printed the leftmost 6 characters in the string named S$.

MID$ printed 3 characters in the string named S$, starting with the 8th character from the left. (Count 'em.)

RIGHT$ printed the 4 rightmost characters in the string named S$.

We added commas after lines 6Ø and 7Ø in order to print everything on one line.

Let's move some lines around to exercise our new-found power. Move line 7Ø to line 5Ø:

```
5Ø PRINT MID$(S$,8,3),
```

and we get

```
WAS                KILROY           HERE
```

Now move line 8Ø to line 4Ø and add a trailing comma

```
4Ø PRINT RIGHT$ (S$,$),
```

and we get

```
HERE               WAS              KILROY
```

These 3 functions can really do wonders with strings. Let's enter a NEW program and examine each in more detail:

```
1 CLS : PRINT

10 FOR N = 1 TO 15

20 PRINT "N = ";N,

30 S$ = "KILROY WAS HERE"

40 PRINT LEFT$(S$,N)

50 FOR T=1 TO 500 : NEXT T

60 NEXT N

90 PRINT : LIST

       and RUN
```

The "slow motion" picture tells it faster than we can in words. LEFT$ picks off "N" letters from the left side of string, and we PRINT them. See how this could be used to strip off only the first 3 digits of a phone number, or the first letter of a name, when searching and sorting?

Change line 10 to read:

```
10 FOR N = 1 TO 20

       and RUN
```

As we see, even though there are only 15 characters in the string, the overrun is ignored. (Change line 10 back to N=1 TO 15.)

RIGHT$ works the same way, but from the right:

Change line 4∅ to read:

```
4∅ PRINT RIGHT$(S$,N)
```

      and RUN.

It's the mirror image of LEFT$.

Now let's exercise MID$ and see where it goes. Change line 4∅ to:

```
4∅ PRINT MID$(S$,N,1)
```

      and RUN.

It very methodically scanned the string, from left to right, picking out one letter at a time. Again we slowed it down with the delay loop in line 5∅ to better understand what's happening.

With only a slight change we can make MID$ act like LEFT$. Change line 4∅ to:

```
4∅ PRINT MID$(S$,1,N)
```

      and RUN.

It printed N characters, counting from number 1 on the left.

MID$ can also simulate RIGHT$. Change line 4∅:

```
4∅ PRINT MID$(S$,16-N,N)
```

      and RUN.

Would you believe RIGHT$ backwards, one at a time?

```
4Ø PRINT MID$(S$,16-N,1)
```

and RUN.

How about a sort of "histogram" type graph:

```
4Ø PRINT MID$(S$,N,N)
```

and RUN.

(Make your notes in the right hand column for future reference. If all these examples don't spark some ideas for your future use, I give up.)

Let's select a specific position in the string and print its character? Make the program read:

```
1 CLS : PRINT

1Ø INPUT"WHICH CHARACTER # DO YOU WANT
                         TO PRINT";N

3Ø S$ = "KILROY WAS HERE"

4Ø PRINT MID$(S$,N,1)

5Ø FOR T = 1 TO 5ØØ : NEXT T

9Ø PRINT : LIST
```

and RUN.

Just to make the point, we can assign any of these statements to a variable. That variable can in turn be used in tests against other variables. Change:

```
4Ø V$ = MID$(S$,N,1)

45 PRINT V$
```

and RUN.

A short book could be written about these 3 functions, but I think we've made the point.

These 3 functions are used frequently in fairly complex sort and select routines. If we remember that they are really very simple, and dissect these routines into their simple parts, they can be understood. The next section is a good example.

INSTRING Routine

INSTRING is not an intrinsic function. It is a routine made up of LEN and MID$, and can be of value when searching for a needle in a haystack. It compares one string against another to see if they have anything in common.

Let's suppose we have a list of names and want to see if another name (or part of that name) is in our list. It's the "part of" which makes this operation very different from a straight comparison of name-against-name, which we already know how to do with ordinary string-against-string comparisons. Here we learn how to locate a name (and similar names) by asking for even a small part of it.

Let's start our program by entering the list of Names:

```
10000 DATA SMITH, JONES, FAHRQUART, BROWN,
                                    JOHNSON

10010 DATA SCHWARTZ, FINKELSTEIN, BAILEY,
                        SNOOPY, JOE BFTSPLK,*
```

That was the easy part.

Now we have to provide a means of READing these names, one at a time and comparing them, or parts of them, with the name or part of a name which we INPUT. Add these lines:

```
10  CLEAR 100 : CLS

20  INPUT"ENTER THE NAME YOU ARE SEEKING "
                        ;N$ : PRINT

30  READ D$

40  IF D$ = "*" PRINT "END OF SEARCH" : END

50  GOSUB 1000

60  IF T = 0 GOTO 30

70  PRINT N$;" IS PART OF ";D$

80  GOTO 30
```

Now this takes a bit of explaining:

Line 10 CLEARs 100 bytes for strings, and CLS the screen

Line 20 INPUTs the name, or part of the name you are trying to locate, and prints a blank space for easier reading to give this book some class.

Line 3Ø READs a single name from our DATA file

Line 4Ø checks to see if we're at the end of the DATA file. If so, it says so and ENDs execution.

Line 5Ø shoots us to the INSTRING subroutine (covered next) which does all the sorting.

Line 6Ø checks the value of T, a number sent back from the subroutine. If its value is Ø it means no such name (or part) was found, and we should READ the next one. If it was found, we drop to

Line 7Ø which PRINTs both what we're looking for and what we found.

Line 8Ø sends us back to READ another name from DATA.

That last part of the program isn't nearly as shaggy as the sort routine itself. Enter these final 3 lines:

```
1ØØØ FOR T = 1 TO LEN(D$) - LEN(N$)

1Ø1Ø IF N$ = MID$(D$,T,LEN(N$)) RETURN

1Ø2Ø NEXT T : T=Ø : RETURN
```

RUN it a few times to get the hang of what's going on, then we'll take it apart.

Line 1ØØØ starts off by setting up a FOR-NEXT loop. How far that loop continues depends on what number comes out of the difference between the length of D$ (from the DATA line) and the length of N$ (the name or part we entered). Even if that number comes out zero or negative, we'll still go through the next 2 lines at least once.

Line 1Ø1Ø is of the IF-THEN variety. If the characters we
INPUT in N$ are the same as the characters taken from
D$, we RETURN to line 6Ø. LEN(N$) **counts** the number of characters we INPUT, so MID$ can take the same
quantity from D$. T gives MID$ the starting point to
count from.

At line 6Ø, we know T will **not** equal Ø since we just said
it equalled 1 in line 1ØØØ. Execution will therefore fall
through to line 7Ø which PRINTS the good news that
we have a "match". Line 3Ø starts the search process
over again in another DATA name, looking for other
possible matches.

If, on the other hand, we did **not** get a match in line 1Ø1Ø
(by far the most frequent event), execution falls through to
line 1Ø2Ø.

Line 1Ø2Ø increments T by one digit, and execution returns
to line 1ØØØ, dropping to line 1Ø1Ø. 1Ø1Ø again tests
our INPUT against the same name READ from DATA,
but this time the starting point, T, moves over by one
place, and a different set of characters is selected. The
same scenario as before repeats.

Eventually the FOR-NEXT loop runs out of T's, and line
1Ø2Ø moves to its next statement, T—Ø. T=Ø sets up a
signal for line 6Ø that the FOR-NEXT loop has run its
course and it's time to READ a new name from DATA.
The RETURN in 1Ø2Ø returns execution back to line
5Ø, then 6Ø.

Now that wasn't too bad, was it? ('Twarnt nothin', really.) A
little time beside the pool reflecting on the logic will do
wonders.

For those with only a silver fingerbowl, but no pool, this extra line will show the inner machinations of line 1000.

```
1005 PRINT"T=";T,"LEN(D$)=";LEN(D$),"LEN(N$)="

;LEN(N$),"DIFF=";LEN(D$) - LEN(N$)
```

Run it through a number of times, halting executing as necessary. It really does make sense!

When you've got that one under control, take out line 1005 to cut down the clutter. Better yet, go into Editor and place a single ' at the beginning of 1005, making it a REM line which can be converted back to a working program line without having to retype it.

Now add line 1007 to show what 1010 is doing.

```
1007 PRINT"T=";T,"N$=";N$,"THE MID$=";
          MID$(D$,T,LEN(N$)),"D$=";D$
```

and RUN.

This one really tells a story! Step right up and see for yourself! Does the string you INPUT really match up with what MID$ is pulling out? Can there be any doubt? How green was my valley? *Hey, who's the fool who's asking all these silly questions?*

It doesn't matter how hard a program seems, when broken down to its individual parts it isn't very hard. Like we've pointed out before, "The BASICs Are Everything".

On The Lighter Side

The specialized string functions allow us to do all sorts of
exotic things. Here is the beginning of a simple but fun program which uses LEN and MID$. You can easily figure it out,
especially after you've seen it RUN.

Enter:

```
1 REM * TIMES SQUARE BILLBOARD *

10 CLEAR 400

20 CLS:N=0:PRINT:READ A$

30 L=LEN(A$) : F=1

80 IF L>N THEN L=N+2

90 B$ = MID$(A$,F,L)

100 PRINT@510-N,;B$

110 FOR T=1TO20 : NEXT T

190 IF N=55 GOTO 220

200 N=N+1 : IF N<55 GOTO 290

220 L=L-1 : F=F+1 : IF L<0 THEN L=0

230 IF L=15 GOTO 20

290 CLS : GOTO80

500 DATA ". . . LUCKY LINDY HAS LANDED
                    IN PARIS . . ."

510 DATA ". . . MET BY LARGE CROWD AT
                LEBOURGET AIRPORT . . ."
```

and RUN.

167

Your assignment, if you choose to accept it, is to complete the program so it repeats, ends, or otherwise does not crash. Good luck! . . . Fssssss!

NOTES

CHAPTER 14

INKEY$

The INKEY$ (pronounced Inkey-string) Function is a powerful one which enables us to INPUT information via the keyboard without having to use the **ENTER** key.

Type this program:

```
1 CLS

10 IF INKEY$="T"THEN 30

20 GOTO 10

30 PRINT"YOU HIT THE LETTER 'T'"

40 GOTO 10
```

and RUN

The keyboard seems to be dead, until you hit the 'T' key. The test in line 10 then passes, execution moves to line 30 and a message is printed. Then the process starts over.

The INKEY$ function glances at the keyboard for only an instant, much like a room is illuminated by a flash bulb or strobe light. Whatever is happening at that time is acted upon. In order to keep the "strobe" flashing as fast as possible, we put INKEY$ into a loop (lines 10 and 20) and keep it "circling" in a "holding pattern" over the keyboard. If we press a key when INKEY$ isn't looking, it will miss us and we'll have to do it again. Press the T key a number of times and note that INKEY$ will occasionally miss your call.

INKEY$ can only "photograph" one letter or number for each flash of the "strobe". If we want to test for more than one character we must write the program to test for each one in sequence. In so doing however, INKEY$'s reliability deteriorates badly.

Add these lines to the program:

```
15 IF INKEY$="P"THEN5Ø

5Ø PRINT"YOU HIT THE LETTER 'P'": GOTO 1Ø
```

and RUN.

As you see, the "miss" rate is much higher. Unless our keystroke matches the timing of the strobe, we won't be seen.

If INKEY$ scans the keyboard and does not find a pressed key (the usual case), it is said to read a "null string". INKEY$ **is** a string function, and null means *nothing*. A null string is represented by two quote marks with nothing between them, thus:

```
" "
```

The ASCII code for null is Ø.

To see how fast the scanning takes place, try this NEW program:

```
2Ø K$ = INKEY$ : PRINT,,,K$ : IF K$ = ""GOTO 5Ø

3Ø GOTO 2Ø

5Ø PRINT "NOTHING FOUND ON THE KEYBOARD" : GOTO 2Ø
```

and RUN

Type in random characters and see them break the scan. Turn on TRON briefly to watch the execution path.

INKEY$ can actually scan much faster than what we see here, but when the scanning loop is burdened down with extra tests and PRINT statements, it makes the distance around the race track longer. In its optimum form, INKEY$ should have the shortest possible scanning loop for highest speed.

You were wondering why we introduced K$ in the above program, when INKEY$ can be printed and tested all by itself, weren't you? Good thinking! Now, shown to the public for the first time in this daring exposé, the startling truth about INKEY$ is revealed. (Hey — Turn off that fool TV set!)

Enter this NEW program:

```
1Ø PRINT INKEY$,INKEY$,INKEY$,INKEY$ : GOTO 1Ø
```

Now, at first blush you might think that an INKEY$ is an INKEY$, so if you type a character it should be printed 4 times.

RUN it.

Aha! It didn't work! That must mean that all 4 INKEY$ are different. What a revolting development this is!

In our search for the lost string, change the program:

```
1Ø A$=INKEY$ : PRINT A$,A$,A$,A$ : GOTO 1Ø
```

and RUN

Aha again! Now we're getting somewhere. By setting a "regular" string variable equal to INKEY$, we can store its value (if briefly) and process it much more efficiently and predictably.

Get the general idea of how to use INKEY$? So simple, yet the possibilities are enormous. Only a lot of experimenting will make you comfortable with it, but INKEY$ will keep you awake nights staring at the ceiling thinking of ways to put it to work.

Out of the blue of the Western Sky . . .

While chasing the solitude needed to write this book, your author flew a heavily loaded light plane, packed with a typewriter, a customized TRS-80 with accessories, plus luggage (and of course, Ham radio) into a medium sized city airport. Transferring this freight to a car turned out to be a big deal since security wouldn't let a car on the apron to off-load the plane. (You're supposed to drop it by parachute?) After some cajoling (and a gratuity) it was agreed that my car could be driven up *near* the apron, and an "officially approved" car could haul the goodies from the plane to the car. It all seemed a bit officious, but election time wasn't close enuf, so . . .

Anyway, to get my car thru the security fence it was necessary to drive to an electrically operated gate and punch a secret code into a numeric keypad for some sort of computer to analyze, and automatically open the gate. The secret code number was 193Ø.

Needless to say, as soon as the TRS-80 was set up I had to write a BASIC program to do everything but actually open the gate. It provides a good example of a real-life application of INKEY$, and is offered here for your amusement, amazement and study.

```
1Ø CLS:PRINT@79Ø, "TYPE THE COMBINATION"

2Ø PRINT@854,;"FOLLOWED BY A PERIOD"

3Ø PRINT@147, "THE ELECTRIC GATE IS CLOSED"

4Ø K$ = INKEY$ : IF K$ = "" GOTO 4Ø

5Ø READ D$ : IF D$ = "." GOTO 1ØØ

6Ø D$ = K$ GOTO 4Ø

7Ø RESTORE : GOTO 4Ø

1ØØ REM * SEE 'CONTROLLING THE WORLD
                 WITH YOUR TRS-80' *
```

```
11Ø REM * BY YOUR FAVORITE AUTHOR FOR
              DETAILS ON HOW *

12Ø REM * TO ACTUALLY OPEN AND
         CLOSE THE ELECTRIC GATE *

13Ø CLS : PRINT@133, "YOU MAY ENTER NOW -
         WAIT FOR THE ELECTRIC GATE TO OPEN"

14Ø FOR T=1TO2ØØØ : NEXT T : RESTORE : GOTO1Ø

1ØØØ DATA 1,9,3,Ø,.
```

The password (193Ø followed by a period) is imbedded, a character at a time, in DATA line #1ØØØ. The commas only separate the characters and should not be typed in to open the gate. Line 4Ø holds the magic. It scans the keyboard looking for something besides a null string. If it finds a key pressed, execution drops to line 5Ø.

Line 5Ø READs a piece of DATA. If it happens to be a period (which can only be READ from DATA after each of the other code characters have been READ), execution moves to line 1ØØ where the gate will be caused to open and line 13Ø will tell you to enter the premises.

If, however, the test in line 5Ø does not find a period, execution defaults to the next test, in line 6Ø.

Line 6Ø checks to see if the keyboard character matches up with the character READ from DATA. If so, the first hurdle has been passed and execution returns back to line 4Ø for INKEY$ to await another keyboard character. If the keyboard and DATA characters don't match, the test fails and execution drops to line 7Ø.

Line 7Ø RESTOREs the DATA pointer back to its beginning, and returns execution to line 4Ø to start scanning all over again. The keyboard puncher sees none of this and has no idea if he is making progress towards cracking the code.

Line 14Ø merely allows the gate a brief time to open and close (and you to read the screen), then RESTOREs the DATA and starts the program over again from the beginning.

The password can be changed to any combination of characters by changing line 1000.

If you wanted it to be 'TRS-80' for example:

    1000 DATA T,R,S,-,8,0,.

Or, 'OPENSESAME'

    1000 DATA O,P,E,N,S,E,S,A,M,E,.

Don't forget that last piece of DATA, the period. By changing line 50, of course, you could change that period to anything you wanted.

Happy gate crashing!

NOTES

What
Price
Precision?

Unless otherwise told, Level II BASIC stores variables with an accuracy of 7 digits, and **prints them out accurate to 6.** This is called "single precision" and is more than adequate for most applications.

For large businesses or special scientific applications however, greater accuracy is needed and we have a capability called "double precision". By telling the Computer to go "double precision", it will store numbers to an accuracy of 17 digits, and **print them out accurate to 16.** We pay a price for this precision however, both in the additional memory it takes to store and process big numbers, and the extra time required to do so.

Enter this program:

```
1 CLS : PRINT

2Ø  X = 123456789Ø987654321      (check 'em)

3Ø  Y = .ØØØØØØØØØ123456789       (count 'em)

4Ø  Z = X * Y

5Ø  PRINT X,Y,Z

9Ø  PRINT : LIST
```

and RUN.

Ummm-hmmm. A very large number times a very small number, and the answer — all expressed in Exponential notation. Accuracy clipped to 6 places.

With ease we can convert storage and processing of X, Y and Z to double precision. This is almost too easy:

```
1Ø DEFDBL A- Z
```

DEFDBL stands for "double precision" and A-Z means, "make every variable starting with any letter from A through Z double precision".

Add the line and RUN.

Quite a difference, eh? We did lose a few digits out in the hinterland, but it expanded our accuracy from 6 places to 16. (Did you see the E for exponential change to D for double precision exponential?)

Such a line is terribly wasteful of memory space and time, except in short programs; but fortunately only a few variables really need to be so precise.

Since the letters X, Y and Z are in sequence, we could tell the Computer to handle only those 3 as double precision, and leave all other variables (of which there are none, right now) as single precision. Change line 10 to:

```
1Ø DEFDBL X-Z
```

and RUN.

Same results.

There is a way to override the DEFDBL declaration. Suppose we wanted Z to be printed as just single precision. We can override line 1Ø by changing those lines which contain Z, as follows:

```
4Ø Z! = X * Y

5Ø PRINT X,Y,Z!
```

and RUN.

Our "raw" data and the calculating was held at high precision, but our final answer is printed out with single-precision accuracy — just what we asked for. A very specific declaration (like the ! , which stands for "single precision"), always takes precedence over a global declaration like in line 1∅. (Global means "valid for the entire program" not just one character or one line.)

There's another way to achieve the above results — just change line 1∅ to:

```
1∅ DEFDBL X,Y
```

or

```
1∅ DEFDBL X-Y
```

It is possible to override one "global" DEFDBL declaration with another. DEFSNG will change everything back to single precision. Let's try it:

```
6∅ DEFSNG X-Z
```

```
7∅ PRINT X,Y,Z and RUN.
```

Good Grief — our "single-precision" numbers turned to zeros!

Well, it turns out that X double precision is a completely separate variable from X single precision: it's as different from X as is Y, or any other variable. If we want to use X and Y again as single-precision numbers, we have to go back and assign their values **AFTER** declaring them to be single precision. Hmmmm.

A cheap and dirty way to show the point is to change line 7∅ to

```
7∅ GOTO 2∅
```

and RUN — hitting the **BREAK** key after both double and single precision versions are printed. (Fortunately, there is rarely reason to **redefine** a variable within a program. If necessary, we can do so with conventional string techniques.)

Double Precision, Another Way

Instead of a "global" declaration of accuracy, we can do it one variable at a time. Change the resident program to read:

```
1 CLS : PRINT

2Ø X# = 1234567890987654321

3Ø Y# = .00000000Ø123456789

4Ø Z# = X# * Y#

5Ø PRINT X#, Y#, Z#

9Ø PRINT : LIST
```

and RUN.

Same results as before. The # sign declares that the variable letter preceding it is to be handled as double precision, overriding the implied declaration that it is single precision.

Remember, X# is not the same as X — it is an entirely different variable. Same with Y# and Z#. To prove the point, add

```
1Ø X = 4

6Ø PRINT X
```

and RUN. X and X# were completely separate, weren't they?

Integer Precision

In a few cases, where the numbers at issue are integers (and in the range between −32768 and +32767) execution can be speeded up by declaring them to be integers using the % sign or the DEFINT statement. Enter this NEW program:

```
2Ø FOR N = 1 TO 5ØØØ

3Ø NEXT N

9Ø PRINT : LIST
```

        and RUN.

Using a stopwatch or clock with a second hand, measure the time it takes the 5ØØØ passes. Should be around 13½ seconds.

Now let's declare N to be an Integer, which is all the accuracy we need, and time it again. Add:

```
1Ø DEFINT N
```

        and RUN.

Aha! It took only about 9½ seconds. That's an increase from about 37Ø passes per second to about 525. A very significant difference.

We can accomplish the same thing using specific declarations. Change the program to read:

```
2Ø FOR N% = 1 TO 5ØØØ

3Ø NEXT N%

9Ø PRINT : LIST
```

        and RUN. Using this method, it runs even faster, coming in at about 9.1 seconds, or 55Ø passes per second.

183

Some Caveats

The Computer makes assumptions. If a constant is written with 8 or more digits, or written in exponential with a "D", it is automatically stored as double precision. When that or any other double-precision number is used in a calculation, the entire calculation will be performed as though **all** numbers involved are double precision. This isn't necessarily bad, but an answer with lots of digits is no more precise than its least accurate ancestors.

Division is unique. All division is done with single precision, regardless how we declare the numerator and denominator. If high accuracy is needed and division is required it's best to substitute multiplication instead, if possible.

If a plain old number falls within the range of −32768 to +32767, or, if it contains a decimal point, or, if it is written in exponential with an "E", it will be stored with single precision. Otherwise, it is stored as an integer.

Finally, logical operations can be performed only with integers.

Degrees of precision may not be the most inspiring subject, nor seem to be the most consistent. But, if we're at least aware of them we'll not be caught off guard and be deceived by numbers that never were. *(Seems to be a lot of those type around . . . eh?)*

NOTES

PRINT USING

Of all the various ways we can PRINT, the most powerful (but most confusing) is the one called PRINT USING. The name PRINT USING itself implies that you *PRINT* something *USING* something else. That implication is correct.

As originally developed for use on large computers, PRINT USING consists of two parts — PRINT and USING. PRINT does as the name implies, USING the format (called the "image") found in **another** line. The TRS-80 PRINT USING is similar, but does not always require a second line for the "image" . . . as we will see.

PRINT USING With Numbers

Type:

```
1Ø  A=123.456789

4Ø  U$ = "###.##"

5Ø  PRINT USING U$;A

        and RUN.
```

The answer is PRINTed as

```
123.46
```

It was rounded up and PRINTed to an accuracy of 2 decimal places.

Add:

```
2Ø  B=1.6

6Ø  PRINT USING U$;B

        and RUN.
```

The screen shows

    123.46

    1.6Ø

The first thing to note is that we have called upon line 4Ø, our image line, twice — once in line 5Ø and again in line 6Ø. Next, note that two answers appeared with their decimal points lined up. Last, see that a Ø has been added to the 1.6 to make it read 1.6Ø. These latter two points are important if you're printing out business reports.

One more addition:

    3Ø C = 9876.54321

    7Ø PRINT USING U$;C

Produces:

    123.46

     1.6Ø

  %9876.54

            What gives ???

Well, the % sign means we have overrun our image lines capacity to print digits **left** of the decimal point, but it prints them anyway. Better to lose our decimal point lineup than important numbers, but it does call our attention to a programming problem. Let's add another # sign to make room for that extra digit. (We are adding another **element** to the **field** in the **image** line. Got that?)

    4Ø U$ = "####.##"

            and RUN.

That's better — but the overrun message would appear again if we tried to print a number with more than 4 digits on the left.

So far, this PRINT USING business looks like it might have some potential, lining up decimal points like it does. We don't have any other reasonable, straightforward way to accomplish that, and it's essential for printing dollars and cents in business reports. Wonder how we can print a dollar sign?

Let's change our image line to:

```
4Ø  U$  =  "$####.##"          (count 'em carefully)
```

　　and RUN.

Nice, eh? The dollar signs all line up in a row:

```
$  123.45

$     1.6Ø

$9876.54
```

But suppose we want the dollar signs to snug right up against each dollar amount? Make 4Ø read:

```
4Ø  U$  =  "$$###.##"
```

　　and RUN

and we get:

```
$  123.46

⊬     1.6Ø

$9876.54
```

　　not specially attractive in this format, but taken singly, as when writing checks, it's almost essential.

The lessons so far are:

1. PRINT USING with # prints the decimal point at the same place for every size number printed.

2. It rounds off the cents (the numbers to the right of the decimal point) to the number of # signs there. It does not round off dollars (left of the decimal point), but sends up an error flag %, prints all dollars, and slips the decimal point to the right if the field isn't large enough.

3. If a single $ is added to the left, dollar signs will be printed and lined up in a column like decimal points. This single $ does not expand the field.

4. If two $ are placed on the left, one $ will be printed on each line and will be placed immediately in front of the first dollar digit. One of these $ can replace one # in the field, thereby not expanding it.

We've covered a lot with very little program, but have a long way to go.

Printing Checks

When using a printer for writing checks, it's usually wise to take extra precautions against "alterations". This is easily accomplished by changing line 4∅ to read:

```
4∅  U$  =  "**###.##"                    (count 'em)
```

The RUN now reads:

```
**123.46

***1.6∅

*9876.54
```

That's swell, it fills up the unused spaces alright, but we lost the dollar sign. Okay, we'll expand the image "field" by one space and put in a dollar sign.

    4Ø U$ = "**$##.##"   (aren't you glad we have an
                            Editor for all these changes?)

See it Now:

    **$123.46

    ****$1.6Ø

    *9876.54

        just like they do it uptown!

If you want to really impress others with the size numbers you usually deal with at your lemonade stand, add lots more # signs to the image line, thus:

    4Ø U$ = "**$##############.##"

and your checks read:

    *************$123.46

    **************$1.6Ø

    ************$9876

        . . . very impressive.

Since we're obviously big time operators, having franchised our lemonade stands, it's getting hard to keep track of the big numbers. How about some commas to break them apart? (Knock out those extra *'s first. Too hard to count them.)

    4Ø U$ = "**$,##.##"   (look closely)

        and RUN.

```
***$123.46

*****$1.65

*$9,876.54
```

Only one of our numbers has more than 3 digits, but a comma separated its 9 and 8 for easier readability. In the image field, the comma can be placed anywhere between the $ and the decimal point, and only **one** comma is required to automatically insert commas to the left of every 3rd digit left of the decimal point. (You really big time operators who deal in the millions will have to wait till the next chapter to see how to go "double precision" to avoid losing the loose change.)

Stringing it out

Let's rework our resident program to show some other PRINTUSING capabilities:

```
1 CLS : PRINT

1Ø A = 123.456789

2Ø B = 1.65

3Ø C = 9876.5432

4Ø U$ = "#####,##      #####,##      #####,##"

5Ø PRINT USING U$;A,B,C

9Ø PRINT : LIST
```

Don't mind lines 1 and 9Ø. They are just handy for clearing the screen, bringing the printout down a space, then LISTing the program for study after it has been printed. I use the technique all the time. You might like it too.

Anyway, RUN it and see how the same numbers can be displayed horizontally instead of vertically. All depends on what you need at a given time.

123.46   1.6Ø   9876.54

PRINT USING With Strings

Change the program to read:

```
1 CLS : PRINT

1Ø A$ = "IT'S"

15 B$ = "HOWDY"

2Ø C$ = "DOODY"

25 D$ = "TIME"

4Ø U$ = "%%"

5Ø PRINT USING U$;A$

9Ø PRINT : LIST
```

and RUN.

The only thing unique about this program is in line 4Ø. As if we didn't already have enough uses for the % sign to worry about, here is another. % is a symbol in TRS-80 PRINT USING which is to strings something like what the # is to numbers.

We used two %% so reserved two spaces for strings, and only IT was printed. Unlike # however, to add more spaces in the string field, we add spaces between the % signs. Change line 4Ø to

```
4Ø U$ ="%  %"
```

and RUN. 4 spaces are set aside and IT'S is printed without clipping.

Let's make room for printing another string on the same line.

```
4Ø U$ = "% %%    %"

5Ø PRINT USING U$;A$,B$
```

and RUN.

Oops! We ran

```
IT'SHOWDY
```

together.

To space them apart we must have to put an actual space in the image field just as we did earlier with printing the numerics.

```
4Ø U$ = "%   %  %    %"
```

and RUN.

That's more like it.

Now it's your turn. Complete lines 4Ø and 5Ø to print IT'S HOWDY DOODY TIME all on one line.

- -

ANSWER:

```
4Ø U$ = "%   %%    %%    %%   %

5Ø PRINT USING U$;A$,B$,C$,D$
```

It's time to quit doodling around and get down to business too! Let's change out HOWDY DOODY for some typical report headings.

```
1 CLS : PRINT

10 A$ = "PART NUMBER"

15 B$ = "DATE PURCHASED"

20 C$ = "DESCRIPTION"

25 D$ = "COST"

40    (you figure out this one yourself)

50 PRINT USING U$;A$,B$,C$,D$

90 PRINT :LIST
```

ANSWER:

```
40 U$ = "% 9 spaces %        %              %
                      %       %      %      % %"
```

(There should be 4 spaces between the %'s where we had to split the line.)

Bring On the Money Changers

Here is a straightforward user program which uses PRINT
USING in a practical way. One would be hard pressed to get
the same results in so short a program without USING it. If
you're not in the international currency business, just type in
the first half-dozen or so DATA lines (plus the last one) to
get a feel for what PRINT USING can do, and see how # & %
can be mixed with blank spaces on the same image line.

```
1 REM   * INTERNATIONAL MONEY CHANGER *
2 REM   * EXCHANGE RATES AS OF AUGUST 1979 *
10 CLS
80 RESTORE : PRINT
100 INPUT"      HOW MANY DOLLARS DO YOU WISH TO EXCHANGE "; D
110 PRINT : PRINT TAB(18); "AT TODAYS RATE YOU WILL GET" : PRINT
400 READ A$, A, B$, B : IF A$="END" THEN 80
460 P$="%                %  ########. ##    %                %  ########. ##"
470 PRINTUSING P$; A$; D/A; B$; D/B
800 C=C+1 : IF C = 11 GOTO 900
850 GOTO 400
900 FOR T=1TO500 : NEXT T : C=0 : PRINT :GOTO400
1000 DATA ARGENTINE PESO, .0007
1010 DATA AUSTRALIAN DOLLAR, 1. 1295
1020 DATA AUSTRIA SCHILLING, .0751
1030 DATA BELGIAN FRANC, .0342
1040 DATA BOLIVIAN PESO, .095
1050 DATA BRAZIL CRUZEIRO, .375
1060 DATA BRITISH POUND, 2. 2360
1070 DATA CANADIAN DOLLAR, .8532
1080 DATA CHILEAN PESO, .0284
1090 DATA COLOMBIAN PESO, .0284
1100 DATA DANISH KRONER, .1902
1110 DATA EGYPTIAN POUND, 1. 45
1120 DATA ECUADORIAN SUCRE, .0357
1130 DATA FINNISH MARKKAA, .2622
1140 DATA FRENCH FRANC, .2347
1150 DATA GREEK DRACHMA, .0276
1160 DATA DUTCH GUILDER, .4975
1170 DATA HONG KONG DOLLAR, .1939
1180 DATA INDIAN RUPEE, .1263
1190 DATA INDONESIAN RUPIAH, .0016
1200 DATA IRANIAN RIAL, .01379
1210 DATA IRISH POUND, 2. 0650
1220 DATA ISRAEL POUND, .0385
1230 DATA ITALIAN LIRA, .001224
1240 DATA JAPANESE YEN, .004619
```

```
1250 DATA JORDIANIAN DINAR, 3.3613
1260 DATA KUWAIT DINAR, 3.6331
1270 DATA LEBANESE POUND, .3082
1280 DATA MEXICAN PESO, .0439
1290 DATA N. ZEALAND DOLLAR, 1.0180
1300 DATA NORWEGIAN KRONER, .1994
1310 DATA PERUVIAN SOL, .004388
1320 DATA PHILIPPINE PESO, .1370
1330 DATA PORTUGAL ESCUDO, .0205
1340 DATA SAUDI ARAB RIYAL, .2976
1350 DATA SINGAPORE DOLLAR, .4660
1360 DATA S. AFRICAN RAND, 1.1928
1370 DATA SPANISH PESETA, .0151
1380 DATA SWEDISH KRONOR, .2374
1390 DATA SWISS FRANC, .6042
1400 DATA TURKISH LIRA, .0212
1410 DATA URAGUAY NEW PESO, .1372
1420 DATA VENEZUELA BOLIVAR, .2330
1430 DATA W. GERMAN MARK, .5468
1500 DATA END,0,END,0
```

PRINT USING

Round 2

In the previous chapter we taught you almost everything you really need to know about PRINT USING. Here are a few other "tricks" that some of you might find helpful.

When printing big bucks (over 999,999 dollars) it is necessary to use double precision or we lose the loose change. Type:

```
1 CLS : PRINT

1Ø A$ = "$$###,######.##"

2Ø D = 123456789.Ø1

3Ø PRINT USING A$;D

9Ø PRINT : LIST
```

   and RUN.

Sure enough, we get $123,457,000.00. Granted, it's only a few minutes interest on the national debt. For businesses doing the *tax***paying** however, the accuracy can be easily improved by simply switching to double-precision. Change lines 2Ø and 3Ø to

```
2Ø D# = 123456789.Ø1

3Ø PRINT USING A$;D#
```

   and RUN.

There it is — $123,456,789.01 — enough change left over to tip the porter who hides the public baggage carts. Notice that the image line didn't have to change. All we did was use a technique we learned in an earlier Chapter.

If the 16-place accuracy of double precision isn't adequate to keep track of the Krugerrands in your mattress, you and Scrooge McDuck can probably afford to spring for a bigger computer.

Profit, or Loss?

Was that healthy number this quarter's **profit** from the lemonade stand, or was it a **loss**? We can make the image line print either. Change it to read:

```
1Ø A$ = "+$$###,######.##"
```

and RUN.

Very nice. Wonder what happened if D was a negative number in line 2Ø?

```
2Ø D# = -123456789.Ø1
```

and RUN

So far, so good. Suppose we take the + out of the image line. Wonder if it will print the negative figure anyway? Use the Editor and take it out.

Then RUN.

Oh, Phsaw! It goofed it up. Must be the + sign adds an element to the image, and the sign takes up that extra place. Well, now we know.

Let's put the + sign back in, this time at the end of the image.

```
1Ø A$ = "$$###,######.##+"
```

and RUN.

Mmmmm. That's nice. Now let's change D back to a positive number and see what happens.

```
2Ø D# = 123456789.Ø1
```

and RUN.

Very nice. Looks better to have the signs at the end, not interfering with the dollar sign, don't you think?

Most printers don't print deficits in red. How can we tag them so we don't allow the project manager to slip them by us. (We'll just take all + numbers for granted.) Let's try changing the + to a minus and see what happens.

```
1Ø A$ = "$$###,######.##-"
```

and RUN.

Seems normal. How about when it's hit with a negative number.

```
2Ø D# = -123456789.Ø1
```

and RUN.

AHA! Sticks out on the printout like a sore thumb. *Now about this little deficit here, Smythe . . . .*

Deviant Forms of PRINT USING

Here's a full-blown weirdo. Even a contradiction in terms. Would you believe a double-precision number, clipped and expressed in double-precision Exponential notation, in PRINT USING? Even the technical types among us with mismatched socks and a rope for a belt will cringe at that one. We aren't going to bore the business types with the gory details, except for a quick intro for those who like to explore the morbid (or is it moribund?).

Change or add these lines:

```
1Ø A$ = "↑↑↑↑#########################"

2Ø D# = 123456789Ø987654321

22 D = 123456789Ø987654321

3Ø PRINT USING A$;D#

4Ø PRINT USING A$;D
```

and RUN.

What you see is what you get, both in double and single precision. Using the Editor, move the block of 4 up-arrows to the right, one space at a time. Have fun!

More on Strings

There is one more PRINT USING character that has real value. Like so many exotic "upgrades" of BASIC, it does nothing that can't be achieved using other BASIC words, but does it easier. Enter this NEW program:

```
1 CLS : PRINT

2Ø X$ = "ALEXANDER"

3Ø Y$ = "GRAHAM"

4Ø Z$ = "BELL"

5Ø A$ = "! ! %        %"

6Ø PRINT USING A$;X$,Y$,Z$

9Ø PRINT : LIST
```

and RUN.

Who should appear before our very eyes but:

```
A G BELL
```

The ! serves to reserve an element in the field for the **first letter** of the string assigned to it. Very handy when you want the initials and last names of a list of people to line up in a row on a printout.

Inputting the Image

We move farther and farther into the woods as we seek to make BASIC's formatting capabilities resemble the superior (and far more complicated) ones of the FORTRAN language from which it was derived. We can even INPUT the image line, since it is a string. An easy way to see this is by using our resident program, but change line 5Ø to read:

```
5Ø INPUT A$
```

and RUN.

We now have to respond by typing in the image line. (Seems like they're hard enough to create without INPUTting.) The safest one to use is old line 5Ø, so respond to the question mark with:

```
? "! ! %     %"
```

and see

```
A G BELL
```

appear again.

RUN again, this time responding with something like:

```
? "%  %     %  %     %          %"
```

and we should see something like

```
ALEX   GRAH    BELL
```

Try some other inputs and see how fast you get into trouble with TM errors. The down-to-earth value of this particular capability is a little elusive.

Another Short Cut

The final area of PRINT USING worthy of examination is the incorporation of the image line into the PRINT USING line. It requires some care, and has value primarily when only a few variables are to be printed, or only printed once. In most practical applications, the image line is referenced many times during a run, frequently by different PRINT USING lines.

Make a few changes in the resident program so it looks like this:

```
1 CLS:PRINT

2Ø X$ = "ALEXANDER"

3Ø Y$ = "GRAHAM"

4Ø Z$ = "BELL"

6Ø PRINT USING "! ! %     %";X$,Y$,Z$

9Ø PRINT : LIST
```

        and RUN.

We simply did away with A$ and incorporated its elements into a built-in image line, separated from the variables by the semicolon. It does save space, and for short and uncomplicated PRINT USING applications, has value. For the long and complicated ones, it's better to keep the image and PRINT USING lines separate.

FINI

As you've seen, PRINT USING is the most complex of our PRINT statements but by far the most powerful. If you're a serious programmer you should master PRINT USING completely; take our many simple learning examples and expand them into large, useful business routines.

CHAPTER 18

Intrinsic Mathematical Functions

Level II BASIC includes a number of mathematical functions for which we had to use sub-routines at Level I. These math functions are all very straightforward and easy to use, but if your math skills are a bit rusty, you will want to refresh them to fully understand what we're doing. We'll keep everything here at the 9th grade Algebra level so there's no need to panic (unless maybe you're in the 6th grade . . .but even so, just hang on and you'll be OK).

INT(N)

We studied the INTeger function in some detail in the Level I Manual so won't have to cover that ground again. However, INT has been expanded at Level II, and is no longer limited to numbers between −32768 and +32767. Larger numbers are stored and executed with single precision.

FIX(N)

FIX is just like INT, but instead of rounding negative numbers downward, it simply chops off everything to the right of the decimal point.

Try this simple test at the command level:

> PRINT INT(-12345.67)

it will PRINT -12346

> PRINT FIX(-12345.67)

it will PRINT -12345

Which you use depends on what you want.

SQR(N)

The square root function is simple to use.

Type this:

```
1Ø INPUT"THE SQUARE ROOT OF";N

2Ø PRINT "IS ";SQR(N)

3Ø PRINT

4Ø GOTO 2Ø
```

and RUN.

Another way to take the square (or any) root of a number is by using the ♦ up-arrow. It of course means "raised to the power". Finding the square root of a number is the same as raising it to the 1/2 power. Change line 2Ø to:

```
2Ø PRINT "IS ";N♦(1/2)
```

and RUN some familiar numbers.

The same logic which allows us to find the square root with the up-arrow will let us find any other root. (Even the thought of doing that in pre-computer days drove men, *and some women,* mad.) Out of sheer arrogance of power, let's find the 21st root of any number. Change the first two lines:

```
1Ø  INPUT"THE TWENTY-FIRST ROOT OF";N

2Ø  PRINT "IS ";N↑(1/21)
```

and RUN.

Now there is real horsepower! Problem is, how are we sure that the answers are right. Well, it's easy enough to add a few lines that take the root back to its 21st power to find out. Let's clean up the program a bit and make it read:

```
1Ø  INPUT"THE TWENTY-FIRST ROOT OF";N

15  R = N↑(1/21)

2Ø  PRINT"IS ":R

3Ø  PRINT

33  PRINT R;"TO THE 21ST POWER = ";R↑21

36  PRINT

4Ø  GOTO 1Ø
```

and RUN.

They come out pretty close, don't they? This "proof" process might not stand up under rigorous scrutiny, but the answers are correct.

SGN(N)

SGN is a real easy one. Its purpose is to tell whether the **sign** of a number is +, − or if the number is Ø. First let's demonstrate the principle with a simple program, then replace most of the program with the SGN function.

```
1Ø  INPUT"ENTER ANY NUMBER";N

2Ø  IF N<Ø THEN S=-1

3Ø  IF N=Ø THEN S=Ø

4Ø  IF N>Ø THEN S=1

5Ø  PRINT S

6Ø  PRINT : GOTO 1Ø
```

and RUN. Try various positive and negative numbers, plus Ø.

As you see, we are given the **sign** in *sign language*. "1" means "positive", "−1" means "negative" and "Ø" means "zero". That's real handy because the answer is already coded in number form, ready to use in a program that needs to know.

And now that we know how it works, let's eliminate most of the program with one simple line:

```
2Ø  S=SGN(N)
```

Delete lines 3Ø and 4Ø

and RUN.

Same results.

ABS(N)

Absolute value has a lot to do with signs, or without them. The absolute value of any number is the number **without** any signs. If you've forgotten, this program will quickly refresh your memory:

```
1Ø  INPUT"ENTER ANY NUMBER ";N

2Ø  A = ABS(N)

3Ø  PRINT A

4Ø  PRINT

5Ø  GOTO 1Ø
```

and RUN. Try various large and small numbers, positive and negative, and zero.

They all come out as they went in didn't they, except the sign is missing.

LOG(N)

No, a log isn't what you build log cabins out of. But even the swiftest among us have to refresh our memory from time to time to keep all the details straight.

A **log** (logarithm) is an **exponent**. Exponent of what? The exponent of a base. What's a base? A base is the number that a given number system is built on. Aren't all number systems built on 1Ø? 'Fraid not.

$$10^3 = 1000$$

1Ø is the BASE. 3 is the log(exponent) and 1ØØØ is the answer.

(Think it has something to do with "new math", but I was fortunately too old to take it, too young to teach it, and grateful for having missed learning it from those who didn't understand it.)

As if life wasn't complicated enough, the LOG system is centered around what are called **natural** logs. What that means is the subject of another discussion, but we're stuck with it anyway. Natural logs use the number 2.71828 as their base. (Really makes your day, doesn't it!) Some interpreters provide a second LOG option using 1Ø as the base, as in our decimal system, but making the conversion isn't too bad — and we still do have to live with it.

Enter this program:

```
1Ø INPUT"ENTER ANY NUMBER";N

2Ø L = LOG(N)

3Ø PRINT"THE LOG OF";N;"TO THE NATURAL
                        BASE =";L

4Ø PRINT

5Ø GOTO 1Ø
```

      and RUN.

Ummm Hmmm. Can't relate to the answers? Enter the number 1ØØ and you should get the answer 4.6Ø517. What it means is, 2.71828 to the 4.6Ø517 power = 1ØØ. Lay that one on them at the next meeting of the Audubon Society and they'll think you're weird for sure.

Let's jack this thing around to where the vast majority of us who have to work with LOGs can use it . . . into the decimal system.

Decimal-based Logs are called "common" logs. Add this line:

```
35 PRINT"THE LOG OF";N;"TO THE BASE 1Ø
            = ";L * .434295
```

     and RUN, using 1ØØ as the number.

Ahhh! That's more like it. We can all see that 1Ø to the 2nd power equals 1ØØ. It's good to be back on *relatively* solid ground.

The magic conversion rules are:

To convert a natural log to a common log, multiply the natural log times .434295.

To convert a common log to a natural log, multiply the common log times 2.3Ø26.

And that's the name of that tune.

This final program clears it up and lays it out:

```
1Ø  REM * LOGARITHM DEMO *

2Ø  INPUT"ENTER A NUMBER";N

3Ø  PRINT

4Ø  PRINT"THE NUMBER",,"NATURAL LOG",
                      "COMMON LOG"

5Ø  PRINT N,,LOG(N),LOG(N)*.434295

6Ø  PRINT

7Ø  GOTO 2Ø
```

EXP(N)

Sort of the opposite of LOG, is EXP. EXP computes the value of the answer, given the EXPonent of a *natural* log. (Another winner.)

2.71828 raised to the EXP power = the answer

Type in this program:

```
1Ø INPUT"ENTER A NUMBER";N

2Ø A = EXP(N)

3Ø PRINT"2.71828 RAISED TO THE";N;
                "POWER = ";A

4Ø PRINT

5Ø GOTO 1Ø
```

and RUN. You're entering the EXPonent now, so it's easy to get the answers that are too big for the Computer and cause it to *overflow*.

As a benchmark against which to test your program, enter this number:

4.6Ø517

The BASE of the natural log system raised to this power should equal 1ØØ.

If you're this far into logs, you can create your own advanced test programs from here, checking the results against a LOG table. *And if you're not too comfortable with all this . . . try making a log cabin with the remainders!*

NOTES

The Trigonometric Functions

Since this is about as deep as we'll get into mathematics, we're going to assume you know something about trig — at least what was covered in the Level I Manual. It might be a good idea to go back and review the last half of Chapter 25 in the Level I Manual just to come up to speed.

Trigonometry of course deals with triangles, their angles, and the ratios between the lengths of their sides. In the triangle below, the Sine (abbreviated SIN) of angle A is defined as the **ratio** (what we get after dividing) of the **length** of side *a* to the **length** of side *c*. COSine and TANgent are defined similarly:

SIN A = a/c

COS A = b/c

TAN A = a/b

From these relationships, we can find any ratio if we know the corresponding angle. Let's try this simple program:

```
1Ø INPUT"ENTER AN ANGLE BETWEEN Ø AND
                        9Ø DEGREES";A

2Ø S = SIN(A*.Ø174533)

3Ø PRINT"THE SIN OF A";A;"DEGREE ANGLE
                                 IS";S

4Ø PRINT : GOTO 1Ø
```

and RUN.

It really works! Try the old "standard" angles like 45°, 30°, 60°, 90°, 0°, etc.

Unless you're right up to snuff on trig, line 2∅ undoubtedly looks strange. Well, it turns out that most computers think in radians, not degrees (always has to be some nasty twist doesn't there . . .!) A radian is a unit of measurement equal to approximately 57° (heard some of you cringe at that one). In order to convert to degrees — which most of us use, we changed the degrees we INPUT to radians. The SIN function would not work correctly without this conversion.

To convert angles from degrees to radians, multiply the degrees times ∅.∅174533.

To convert angles from radians to degrees, multiply the radians times 57.29578.

Failure to make these conversions correctly is **BY FAR** the greatest source of computer users' problems with the trig functions.

Cosine and Tangent work the same way. Change the resident program to:

```
1∅ INPUT"ENTER AN ANGLE BETWEEN ∅ AND
                      9∅ DEGREES";A

2∅ C = COS(A*.∅174533)

3∅ PRINT"THE COS OF A";A;"DEGREE ANGLE
                            IS";C

4∅ PRINT : GOTO 1∅
```

For Tangent, RUN this program:

```
1Ø INPUT"ENTER AN ANGLE BETWEEN Ø AND
                          9Ø DEGREES";A

2Ø T = TAN(A*.Ø174533)

3Ø PRINT"THE TAN OF A";A;"DEGREE ANGLE
                            IS";T

4Ø PRINT : GOTO 1Ø
```

This next simple program displays all 3 major trig functions at the same time. Note in line 3Ø we **divide** our incoming angle by 57.29577 instead of multiplying it by Ø.Ø174533. The results are the same.

```
1Ø CLS

2Ø INPUT"ENTER AN ANGLE BETWEEN Ø AND
                          9Ø DEGREES";A

3Ø A = A/57.29577

4Ø PRINT

5Ø PRINT"ANGLE","SIN","COS","TAN"

6Ø PRINT A*57.29577,SIN(A),COS(A),TAN(A)
```

The opposite of finding a ratio between two sides of a triangle when an angle is known, is finding an angle when the ratio of two sides is known. There are 3 functions commonly used in trig to do this, but most computers only make provision for one, called ATN (Arc of the TANgent).

This simple program takes the angle we INPUT, computes and PRINTs its TANgent, then takes that tangent and computes the arc (angle) of that tangent. The letter I is used in the program since the arctangent is also known as the "inverse" (sort of the "opposite") of the tangent.

```
1 CLS

1Ø REM * ATN DEMO *

2Ø INPUT"ENTER ANY ANGLE BETWEEN Ø AND
                        9Ø DEGREES";A

3Ø T = TAN(A/57.29578)

4Ø PRINT "TANGENT =";T,

5Ø I = ATN(T) * 57.29578

6Ø PRINT"ARC OF THE TANGENT = ";I
```

If you're one of those rare types who are very familiar with trig you can probably throw numbers around in such a fashion that the other 2 "inverse" trig functions, ARCSIN and ARCCOS are not needed. But for those of us who still get confused when we run out of fingers and toes we can use the following conversions, all built into one simple program. The accuracy is close enough for "government" work. Give it a try:

```
1Ø CLS : REM * INVERSE FUNCTION DEMO
                        PROGRAM *

2Ø INPUT"ENTER A NUMBER - THE RATIO OF
                        2 SIDES";R

3Ø A=ATN(R/SQR(ABS(1.ØØØØØØ1◢R 2))) * 57.29578
```

```
4Ø  C=9Ø - A : PRINT

5Ø  PRINT"RATIO","ARCSINE","ARCCOS","ARCTAN"

6Ø  PRINT"(NUMBER)","(DEGREES)","(DEGREES)",
                                 "(DEGREES)"

7Ø  PRINT R,A,C,ATN(R)*57.29578

8Ø  PRINT : GOTO 2Ø
```

Remember that while the TANgent can be any number from
Ø to nearly infinity, when our ratio (number) moves outside
that range, SIN and COS are both out of the first quadrant.
At that point we've moved out of the scope of this book.
(Good thing — I'm a little bored with it all too . . .)

Graphing TRIG Functions

It is often helpful to graph mathematical functions so we can
better understand what's going on. The TRS-80 graphics are
adequate for a non-precision examination of many mathematical functions, and the following short demo programs
illustrate that capability.

Just imagine there is a coordinate system drawn on the screen
(or draw your own, either with the Computer or a china
marker). The numbers in these demo programs are not magic,
they just allow the graphs to be drawn large, but not so large
they try to run off the screen.

These programs are included to get you started (and to liven up this Chapter). Experiment to get what you want for your own particular application.

Graphing of Single Sine Wave

```
1 CLS : PRINT@Ø,"SINE"

1Ø FOR X = Ø TO 255

2Ø Y = SIN(X/4Ø)

3Ø SET(X/2,2Ø-Y*2Ø)

4Ø PRINT@5Ø,"X=";INT(X/2);

5Ø PRINT@58,"Y=";INT(2Ø)-Y*2Ø);

6Ø NEXT X

7Ø GOTO 7Ø
```

Graph of 3 Cosine Waves

```
1 CLS : PRINT@7,"COSINE"

1Ø FOR X =Ø TO 765

2Ø Y = COS(X/4Ø)

3Ø SET(X/6,2Ø-Y*2Ø)

4Ø PRINT@45,"X=";INT(X/6);

5Ø PRINT@53,"Y=";INT(2Ø-Y*2Ø);

6Ø NEXT X

7Ø GOTO 7Ø
```

Graph of the Tangent

```
1 CLS : PRINT@7"TANGENT"

10 FOR X = 0 TO 126

20 Y = TAN(X/90)

30 SET(X,47-Y*8)

40 PRINT@40,"X=";INT(X);

50 PRINT@48,"Y=";INT(47-Y*8);

60 NEXT X

70 GOTO 70
```

There is obviously quite an education to be had by careful study of the graphs. Look for such things as relative thickness of the line at different points, the rate at which blocks are lit relative to the other variable, etc. Sure beats the "early days" when we had to try and imagine these things on a blackboard.

Multi-Dimension Arrays

In the Level I Manual, we learned that an array is nothing more than a temporary parking area for lots of numbers. Not much has changed, except at Level II we can store either numbers or alphabet characters, or both. In addition, because of the greatly increased string handling capability, we have the ability to compare string contents outside the matrix (or array) with those inside it. At Level I we could only compare numbers with both numeric and string arrays. We have more possible array names now than we could ever use, not just A(N).

An array which only has 1 dimension, that is, just one long line-up of parking places is sometimes called a vector. That's what we had to work with at Level I. We can take that same 1-dimensional array and cut it into, say, 4 equal chunks, and position those chunks side by side. We then call it a 2-dimensional array — since the parking places are lined up in ROWS and COLUMNS (or STREETS and AVENUES). Not a single thing has changed about its DATA holding or processing abilities. Only the addresses of the parking places (or elements or memory cells) has changed.

Enter this program:

```
1Ø DIM M(52)
```

> any array with more than 11 elements (counting Ø) must be DIMensioned.

```
2Ø FOR V = 1 TO 52
```

```
3Ø   PRINT V
```

```
4Ø NEXT V
```

> and RUN

The RUN simply shows us the 52 storage positions and the numbers (addresses) of those positions. They are all lined up in a single row, so can be called a vector. What it didn't show us was the **contents** of those memory cells. Let's change the program and find out what's being stored:

```
30 PRINT M(V)
```

    and RUN.

Hmmmm. Every cell is storing the number ∅. Why? Because every value is initialized at zero on power-up; and by typing RUN, we find this out — just like with all the other numeric or string variables we have encountered at Level II. It's sure nice to know **what** we have to work with, instead of just random numbers floating around . . . a distinct improvement over Level I. Now we know both how to find the **address** of each memory cell, and how to find its **contents**.

Let's now cut our 52 cell array into 4 equal strips, and line them up side by side. That would make . . . ah . . . er . . . 13 rows . . . er . . . each containing 4 cells . . . right? Or 4 columns containing 13 cells. A "2 dimensional array" — has rows and columns. Let's start over with this NEW program:

```
10 DIM M(13,4)
```

    that's 13 rows by 4 columns

```
20 FOR R = 1 TO 13

30   FOR C = 1 TO 4
                R  C
40    PRINT M;M,

50   NEXT C

60 NEXT M  R
```

    and RUN.

And there we see the **addresses** of all 52 cells displayed on the screen at the same time. Again, nothing has changed from the earlier vector array containing the same 52 cells. We just rearranged the furniture and gave it different addresses. They read:

1 1   means "first row, first column

8 3   means "8th row, 3rd column"

      etc.

Now let's find out what each of these cells is holding in the way of DATA. Change line

40   PRINT M(N,H),

      and RUN.

See, the contents remain unchanged. They are still at their initialized value of zero, since we have made no arrangement to store information in them. Isn't this easy (. . . so far)?

Memory cells have to be "loaded" with DATA to be of any value. This can be done by reading the DATA in from DATA lines, by INPUTting it via the keyboard, or from a previously recorded DATA tape. Best of all, it can be input at high speed from a disk, but that's not part of this book. It's covered in *Learning Disk BASIC and TRSDOS*, but we can still load our Matrix from DATA lines imbedded in the program. The results and potential are just not nearly as dramatic.

Add these DATA lines:

```
1ØØ DATA 1,2,3,4,5,6,7,8,9,1Ø,11,12,13,
            14,15,16,.17,18,19,2Ø

11Ø DATA 21,22,23,24,25,26,27,28,29,3Ø,
            31,32,33,34,35,36,37

12Ø DATA 38,39,4Ø,41,42,43,44,45,46,47,
            48,49,5Ø,51,52
```

and this line to READ the DATA and plug it into matrix cells:

```
35 READ M(R,C)
```

and RUN.

There we can see the DATA all nicely arranged in the matrix, and each matrix position has a specific address. Let's stay in the command mode for a minute and "poll" or "interrogate" several matrix positions and see what they are holding. Ask:

```
>PRINT M(2,3)
```

write down 7, the answer. We'll RUN the program again later and check it.

```
>PRINT M(11,4)
```

it says **that** cell holds the number 44

```
>PRINT M(3,5)
```

?BS error? Why did we get that? Oh, there is no column 5. No wonder.

Let's RUN the program again and check the screen, counting down the Rows and over the Columns to see if our answers match up.

Mine did — how about yours?

As an aside, type

    CLEAR

then, at the command level, check any matrix memory spot again.

    > PRINT M(2,2)

        and we get ∅. CLEAR re-initialized all cells to zero, along with all other variables. We can of course reload them by RUNning again.

Okay, Now What Do We Do With It?

Good question. Everything you learned in the Level I User's Manual applies. We've only rearranged the deck chairs on this Titanic (oops, poor choice of vessels . . .) — the end result is unaffected (and it won't sink).

At this point, what we've learned is best utilized for calling up and loading relatively unchanging DATA. It is placed in a matrix so it can be accessed and compared, processed or otherwise put to work. Typical applications are:

1. **Technical tables**. Instead of having to keep looking up the same information in tables, store the tables in DATA lines and let the Computer look them up, do the calculations and give you the final answer. Works great in this application, and the time saved quickly pays for the Computer. If we didn't have the LOG and TRIG functions built in, they would be ideal candidates for storing of table info.

2. I've seen this approach used by a lumber yard to furnish fast quotes on materials, and by a printing shop for fast quoting of all sorts of printed materials. In the latter case, the program is written so simply that the customer bellys right up to the counter, answers the computer's questions, and gets his quote right there on the screen. The latest prices on all the paper products and printing costs are held in DATA lines and "spun up" into the Matrix at the beginning of the day. The customer just responds to a "menu" on the screen, and answers the questions. After the quote is calculated, the menu reappears for the next customer.

When DATA is loaded in externally, either via the keyboard or a DATA tape, we obviously don't want to have to go through **that** loading process each time we want an answer. It's important therefore, not to let execution END. Always have it come back to a screen "menu" of choices, or at least a simple INPUT statement. If an END is hit, the matrix crashes and the DATA has to be reloaded.

String Matrices

So far we have seen only numbers in our arrays. We can also use them to hold letters or words, using the same rules we learned earlier in the Chapters on Strings, including CLEAR-ing enough space for the Strings. We have to give string matrices String names. Make these subtle changes in our resident program:

```
10 DIM M$(13,4)

35  READ M$(R,C)

40 PRINT M$(R,C)
```

and RUN.

Absolutely no difference! We now have a string matrix. The data was all numeric, but it handled it beautifully.

Now let's change our DATA (and cut down the program a bit so we don't have to type so much) and try it again. Change:

```
20 FOR R = 1 TO 6

100 DATA ALPHA, BRAVO, CHARLIE, DELTA,
          ECHO, FOXTROT, GOLF, HOTEL

110 DATA INDIA, JAPAN, KILO, LIMA, MIKE,
          NOVEMBER, OSCAR, PAPA

120 DATA QUEBEC, ROMEO, SIERRA, TANGO,
          UNCLE, VICTOR, WHISKEY

130 DATA XRAY, YANKEE, ZULU
```

and RUN.

Really no difference between the string matrix and the numeric ones before, except the handle letters. Stop for a moment and contemplate the string-comparing and string-handling techniques you learned a few Chapters ago. Your mind should be running flat out at this point, considering the possibilities.

How about mixing strings and numerics?

(Sounds good — I'll have one on the rocks)

Oh! Funny you should ask. That's why we ran all numbers in a string matrix, then all words with that same program. They mix very well, as long as we make it a string matrix and not a numeric one.

We have one final program. It is not meant to be a practical one, but could be expanded to INPUT the DATA from tape (or better, disk) and be quite usable. However, it does demonstrate a few important possibilities and is worth entering and studying:

The Objective

The objective of this demo program is to allow a church treasurer to keep track of who gave what, when. Could do the same thing with a service club, or any organization that has a membership and dues. We want to be able to access every member's record by name, and get a readout on his status.

Let's start the program with the DATA. Type this in the NEW program:

```
1000 REM * DATA FILE *

1010 DATA 07.0179,JONES,15

1020 DATA 07.0179,SMITH,87

1030 DATA 07.0179,BROWN,24

1040 DATA 07.0179,JOHNSON,53

1050 DATA 07.0179,ANDERSON,42
```

Analyzing the DATA, we've employed several techniques. The first number in each DATA line employs "data compression", that is, "encoding" several pieces of information into one number. This number contains the month, date and year in one 6 digit number. (Using string techniques, we could easily strip them apart again if we wished, for special reports.) Single precision will hold the 6 digits accurately.

The second thing we've done with this first number is protect the leading Ø. Since months below October are represented by only one number, the leading zero would be lost on these months and the number changed to only 5 digits. There are other ways to get around that problem, but we will throw in a decimal point just to act as an unmovable reference.

The second element in each DATA line is the name. We could put in the full name, but if we used a comma we'd of course have to enclose the name in quotes.

The third element of each DATA line holds the amount of money given on that date.

Obviously, a full DATA set would contain many entries for each Sunday, and many Sundays in a row. We don't need to enter that much DATA to demonstrate the principles involved so will just keep it short and to the point.

We now have to READ this DATA into a string matrix, displaying it on the screen as we go. Add:

```
5 CLS:PRINT"ENTRY #","DATE","NAME","TITHE $":PRINT

1Ø FOR E = 1 TO 5 : PRINT E, 'THIS SUNDAY'S ENTRY

2Ø   FOR M = 1 TO 3              'MEMBERS NAME

3Ø     T = M                     'WEEKLY TITHE IN $

4Ø       READ R$(E,M,T)

5Ø        PRINT R$(E,M,T),

6Ø     NEXT M

7Ø NEXT E
```

and RUN.

Very good. The Matrix is loaded, and confirmed on the screen. We see the first 5 bookkeeping entries from Sunday, July 1, 1979.

Now that we know it loads OK, we can remove some of the software. Change these lines:

```
1Ø FOR E = 1 TO 5            'THIS SUNDAY'S ENTRY
```

Delete line 5Ø

and RUN.

Good. We still get the heading, but the display is gone. Now, how can we interrogate the Matrix to pull an individual member's record? Guess we first have to ask a question. Type:

```
100 INPUT"WHOSE RECORD ARE YOU SEEKING";N$
```

and RUN.

Seems to work OK. We will just answer the question with any member's name as it appears in the DATA lines. Then we have to scan the matrix and compare N$, the name we INPUT, with each element, R$(E,M,T), until we find a match. This means setting up the FOR-NEXT loops again and scanning every element. Add:

```
110 FOR E = 1 TO 5

120   FOR M = 1 TO 3

130    T = M

140     IF R$(E,M,T) = N$ GOTO 200

150   NEXT M

160 NEXT E : PRINT "NOT IN THE FILE" : GOTO 100

200 PRINT E, R$(E,M-1,T-1),R$(E,M,T),R$(E,M+1,T+1)

210 PRINT : GOTO 100
```

and RUN.

Try names that are in the DATA lines, and those that are not. Lines 160 and 210 have built-in defaults back to the question.

The key line is #2∅∅. It prints 4 things:

E   Obviously the entry number on that date

R$(E,M-1,T-1) not so obviously, the contents of the
memory cell just **preceding** the one containing the
member's name. The name being the center of 3
cells on each DATA line, we must print both it and
the one before it and the one after it.

R$(E,M,T) The cell containing the name

R$(E,M+1,T+1) The cell following it

If you have trouble visualizing what line 2∅∅ is doing, add
this temporary line. It prints the address of each DATA element just below it, and is very helpful:

```
2∅5 PRINT E, E;M-1;T-1, E;M;T, E;M+1;T+1
```

        and RUN

Implications

Again, the preceding program was not written to be a model
of programming style and efficiency — but to be a good
learning program. You should now sit by the bank of the
creek and think through how you would modify it to load in
say, 1∅∅∅ lines of DATA from cassette tape via an INPUT
statement. Then, add more DATA each Sunday and shoot
that updated DATA back out to tape for reuse the following
Sunday, or inbetween as needed. It is possible, and marginal-
ly practical to use your TRS-80 for this application.

By the time you solve the software problems, you will get
some additional encouragement in the Chapter on using Dual
Cassettes.

NOTES

CHAPTER 21

PEEK
and
POKE

PEEK and POKE are BASIC words that allow us to do non-BASIC things. They provide the means whereby we can PEEK into the innards of the Computer's memory, and if we wish, POKE in new information.

It is not our purpose here to become an expert in machine language programming, or even on how the Computer works. We have to approach this and related topics a little gingerly lest we fall over the edge into a computer abyss (or is it an abysmal computer?).

We do know, however, that computers do their thing entirely by the manipulation of numbers. Therefore, when we PEEK at the contents of memory, guess what we'll find? Numbers? Very good! (Ummmyass).

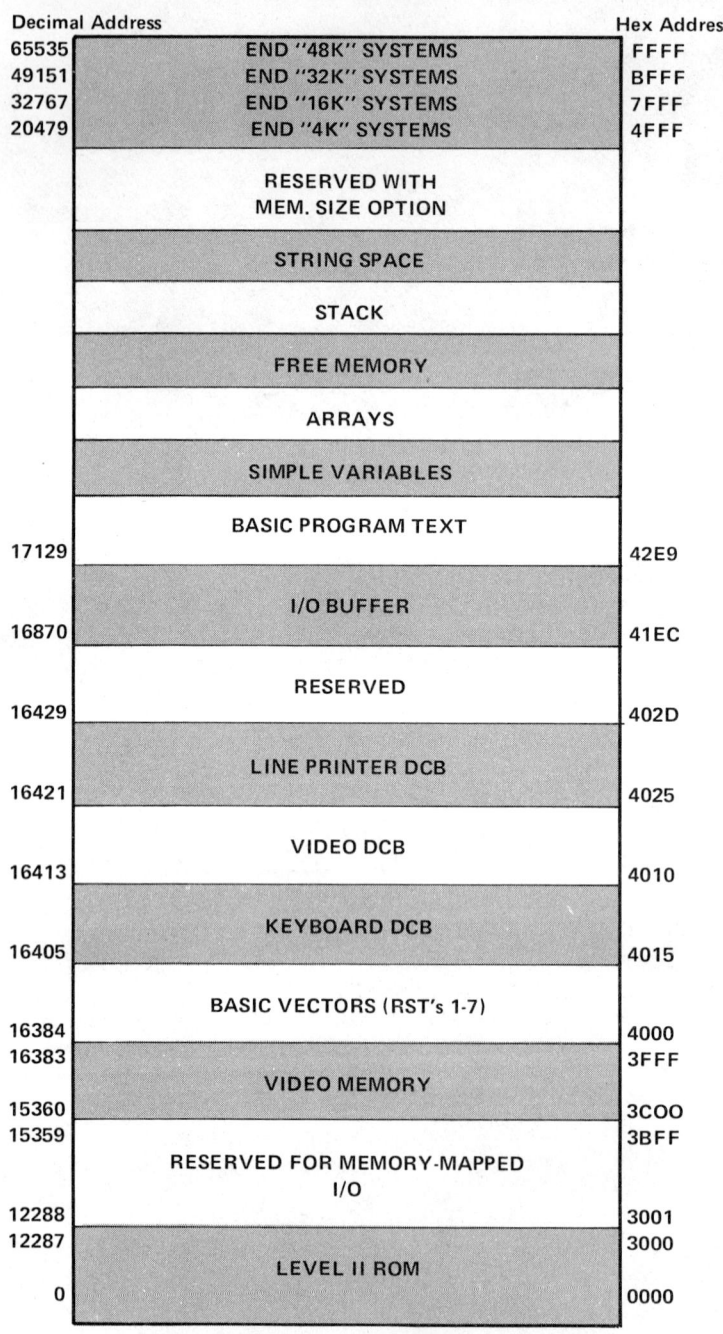

Figure 1. Level II Memory Map

As you can easily see from the Memory Map in Figure 1, large chunks of the Computer's memory are set aside, or "mapped" for very specific uses. (Oh, you can't see it easily . . .? Had your eyes checked lately?) The Level II ROM for example, uses byte addresses 0 through 12287. All numbers we talk about here are decimals, not hex, octal, binary or Sanskrit.

Type in this program:

```
20  N=0

50  PRINT N, PEEK(N), CHR$(PEEK(N))

60  N=N+1

70  GOTO 50
```

Let's analyze the program before RUNning it.

Line 20 sets the beginning address where we want to start PEEKing. As Figure 1 shows, there are lots of good places to go spelunking, and we can change line 20 to start wherever we want.

Line 50 prints three things:

A. The address — that is, the number of the byte, the contents of which we are PEEKing at.

B. The contents of that byte, expressed as a decimal number between 0 and 255.

C. For convenience (and some value), the contents of that address converted to its ASCII character. (Many of the ASCII characters are not printable — we warned you it was a ribald novel.) Go back to the chapter on ASCII if *your* memory has grown dim.

OK, now RUN the program, being ready to stop it with SHIFT@ if you see something interesting. It can also be stopped at any time with the BREAK key, and restarted with CONT without having to start all over again with N at 0.

Didn't see anything interesting? What did you find starting at address 261??? You have to be able to read vertically as the letters swish by.

When the letters jump to double width, hit STOP, then CLEAR, then CONT, as they are too hard to read when so large. Change N to start at different places in memory and PEEK to your heart's delight. You can't goof up anything by just PEEKing. It's indiscriminant POKEing that gets you into trouble.

The command level is very handy for resetting the starting address. Change the value of N by just typing:

    N=5ØØØ

        for example, then

    CONT

        instead of RUN

When done PEEKing with this program and having seen far more information than can possibly be absorbed, rework line 5Ø to read simply

    5Ø PRINT CHR$(PEEK(N));

        .and RUN.

It PRINTs only the ASCII characters, horizontally, and is the ideal program to RUN when friends visit. Just act casual about the whole display and avoid any direct questions. Makes a great background piece for a science fiction movie.

When you find an interesting spot, hit BREAK, then

    PRINT N
        at the command level to find out where in memory you are PEEKing. (Don't you wish you could explore the corners of your mind as easily?)

    CONTinue on when ready.

Having moved from PEEKing to leering, it's time to see what else we can do.

Careless POKEing can leave holes . . .

Before POKEing, we'd better see that we're not POKEing a stick into a hornets' nest. It's with the greatest of ease that we destroy a program in memory by POKEing around where we shouldn't.

Obviously there is no use POKEing in the ROM area since ROM stands for Read Only Memory. It's not changeable. The rest of the "Memory mapped" area, from 12288 thru 17129 is reserved for specific things, so best not to POKE in there while we're just bungling around. Anything above 17129 should be available memory, unless taken up with our BASIC program or required for processing. With such a short program as ours we surely can't goof anything up? Can we?

Let's PEEK around 20000 and see if anything is going on there. Change two program lines to:

```
20 N = 20000

50 PRINT N; PEEK(N),
```

and RUN

Next page, please . . .

20000	255	20001	255	20002	255	20003	255
20004	255	20005	255	20006	255	20007	255
20008	255	20009	255	20010	255	20011	255
20012	255	20013	255	20014	255	20015	255
20016	255	20017	255	20018	255	20019	255
20020	255	20021	255	20022	255	20023	255
20024	255	20025	255	20026	255	20027	255
20028	255	20029	255	20030	255	20031	255
20032	0	20033	0	20034	0	20035	0
20036	0	20037	0	20038	0	20039	0
20040	0	20041	0	20042	0	20043	0
20044	0	20045	0	20046	0	20047	0
20048	0	20049	0	20050	0	20051	0
20052	0	20053	0	20054	0	20055	0
20056	0	20057	0	20058	0	20059	0
20060	0	20061	0	20062	0	20063	0

What we see are the address numbers and their contents, in
easy-to-read parallel rows. Unless you've been messing around
with other programs since power-up, you should just see nice
rows of 255's and 0's. The memory at this location is not
being used.

Great! Let's change our program and POKE in some information and do something with it. Make it read:

```
1Ø  REM  *  POKE  PROGRAM  *

2Ø  N = 2ØØØØ

4Ø  READ D

5Ø  POKE N,D

6Ø  N = N+1

7Ø  IF N = 2ØØ11 END

8Ø  GOTO 4Ø

1ØØ  DATA 8Ø,69,69,75,45,65,45,66,79,79,33
```

Before RUNning, let's analyze it.

Line 2Ø initializes the starting address at 2ØØØØ

Line 4Ø READs a number from the DATA line

Line 5Ø POKEs the DATA "D" into address "N"

Line 6Ø increments the address number by one

Line 7Ø ENDs execution when we have POKEd in all 11 pieces of DATA

Line 8Ø sends us back for more DATA

Line 1ØØ stores the DATA we are going to POKE into memory.

Now – RUN

Well, that was sure fast. I wonder what it did? How can we find out? Should we PEEK at it? Yes, but let's leave the old program in and just start a new one at 200.

```
200 REM * PEEK PROGRAM *

210 FOR N=20000 TO 20010

220 PRINT N, PEEK(N)

230 NEXT N
```

and RUN200

20000	80
20001	69
20002	69
20003	75
20004	45
20005	65
20006	45
20007	66
20008	79
20009	79
20010	33

How about that. We really did change the contents of those memory locations. We shot the numbers from our DATA line right into memory. Now if we only knew what those numbers stood for. Wonder ... if we changed them to ASCII characters, would they tell us anything?

Add:

    2Ø5 CLS

    22Ø PRINT@47Ø+N-2ØØØØ,CHR$(PEEK(N));

        to print at a certain location on the screen

and RUN2ØØ

Print The Results Here

And that's how PEEK and POKE work.

A Study
in Obscurities

SYSTEM

SYSTEM is a BASIC word that lets you get out of BASIC . . . in case you want to. There are some good reasons to, not the least of which is to load in the Keyboard Debounce tape. You may recall in the chapter on Converting Programs from Level I to Level II we used SYSTEM.

Insert the tape titled KEYBOARD DEBOUNCE SYSTEMS * KBFIX in your recorder. (The tape is available free at Radio Shack stores.) Be sure it's fully rewound. Press PLAY, then type:

SYSTEM **ENTER**

the screen will respond with

*?

a sure sign you are at SYSTEM level. (Not the same as BASIC Command Level.)

Type

KBFIX **ENTER**

the name of the machine language program we wish to load. The asterisks will appear plus another

*?

This time we respond simply with

/ **ENTER**

and watch the screen document what is happening.

TRS-80 RELOCATING LOADER.

BASE = BFFF   (or some other HEX number)

KB DEBOUNCE ROUTINE.

LOADING RELOCATION DIRECTORY.

LOADING RELOCATABLE CODE.

RELOCATION COMPLETE, BASE = BFC8

    (or other HEX)

READY

>

It's all very efficient and computer-like.

After we went from command level to SYSTEM level, the tape played in a machine language program which changed the machine language program which controls the keyboard. The change fixed the keybounce problem (if you've had one ... maybe you didn't even know about it), then returned control back to the BASIC command level.

There are other reasons to use SYSTEM than wanting to load machine language tapes — though that is a good one. By using the TRS-80 EDITOR/ASSEMBLER, available through Radio Shack stores, if you are interested, you can create your own high-speed assembly language programs. But, lest we forget, BASIC was created primarily because assembly language progamming is quite confusing (not much English language — a lot of letters and numbers . . . ugh). If you think BASIC is tough — you ain't seen nothin' until you try programming in machine or assembler. An "assembly" language is a low level language which allows the user to create machine programs, but to do so by writing characters instead of all numbers. Assembler is easier to program with than machine (all ones and zeros), but much more difficult than high level languages such as BASIC.

USR

The USR function has a variety of uses, most of them having little to do with BASIC. It allows us to "call" or "gosub" a program written in assembly language, and "return" back to our BASIC program when it's finished. To make much sense of USR you'll need assembly language skills — not a part of this book. You will have a chance to see USR in action in the upcoming chapter dealing with the REAL TIME CLOCK. We use it there almost like a simple toggle switch to turn the clock on and off when we want.

In its simplified form we might think of

    X=USR(1)

          as meaning "turn it on"

and

    X=USR(∅)

          as meaning "turn it off"

What it *actually means* of course is determined by the function of the machine language program it's "calling".

USR in use

Without getting out too deep in the water, memory addresses 16526 and 16527 are inspected by USR to find out where in memory we have stored a machine language program.

If it starts at 32000 for example, we have to express 32000 in Hexadecimal, then split that HEX number into its *least* and *most significant bytes,* convert those bytes separately back to decimal, and POKE that information into 16526 and 16527. *(Are you really sure you want to go through with this?)*

Looking at the HEX-to-Decimal conversion chart, 32000 is readily seen (by any Ace digital engineer) to equal 7530 HEX. We divide 7530 into 30 and 75, the least and most significant bytes respectively. By converting them back to decimal using the same chart, we get:

30 = LSB = 48 decimal

and

75 = MSB = 117 decimal

Ummm-ahhhh-yaas!

Now, we POKE that starting address into our BASIC program, something like this:

```
1Ø POKE 16526,48 : POKE 16527,117
```

and we're set to call our non-existent machine language program at 32000 from BASIC by simply saying:

```
X=USR(1)
```

Suitably impressed? Or, *big deal! . . . ? . . .*

HEX CODE	Most Significant Bytes		Least Significant Bytes	
	IV	III	II	I
Ø	Ø	Ø	Ø	Ø
1	4Ø96	256	16	1
2	8192	512	32	2
3	12288	768	48	3
4	16384	1Ø24	64	4
5	2Ø48Ø	128Ø	8Ø	5
6	24576	1536	96	6
7	28672	1792	112	7
8	32768	2048	128	8
9	36864	23Ø4	144	9
A	4Ø96Ø	256Ø	16Ø	1Ø
B	45Ø56	2816	176	11
C	49152	3Ø72	192	12
D	53348	3328	2Ø8	13
E	57344	3584	224	14
F	6144Ø	384Ø	24Ø	15

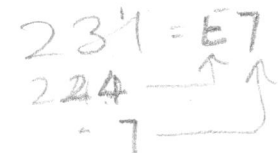

Hex-to-Decimal Conversion Chart

Decimal Value = IV + III + II + I

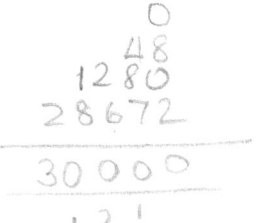

That's as far as we're going to press our luck on this one right now. You'll have a chance to actually do all these good things in the REAL TIME CLOCK chapter, and we don't want to leave you so terror-stricken that you won't get that far.

Machine and Assembly language programming books on the Z-80 are readily available for that small percentage of readers who want to pursue the subject. You at least now have a sufficient introduction to nod your head and smile knowingly when others try to impress you with their knowledge of these things.

INP

The TRS-80 has 256 "ports" or channels of communication with the "outside world". They are numbered from ∅ to 255. Because this whole subject is worthy of an entire book itself, we will only learn enough here to get an elementary "feel" for it.

Only one of these ports in the TRS-80 is specifically assigned a single task. Port number 255 controls the cassette recorder. All other ports are available to take in information or send it out via the bus connector under the access door at the back of the Computer. (Just look now — no fiddling please.)

You're not going to "Control The World" with what you learn about ports in this Chapter, but enter this program and you may be surprised at what INP can do.

CompuSoft Publishing has an excellent book titled *Controlling The World With Your TRS-80* (by your favorite author) which takes the beginner all the way through advanced applications of the TRS-80 using information INPut and OUTput via these 256 ports.

```
1∅ OUT 255,∅

2∅ S = INP(255): PRINT S,

3∅ IF S = 255 GOTO 5∅

4∅ PRINT "NO DATA COMING FROM CASSETTE" :
                              GOTO 1∅

5∅ PRINT,"DATA IS FLOWING FROM CASSETTE" :
                              GOTO 1∅
```

Now, place a program tape in the recorder (BLACKJACK will do nicely). Set the volume where you usually do. Remove the REM motor control plug, and press PLAY. Type RUN.

Haha! Didn't expect that, did you? Here's how it works:

Line 1Ø Disregard for right now

Line 2Ø Looks at port #255 and reads a coded message, then prints that code.

Line 3Ø Tests that code number against the number 255. The number 255 in this program line bears no relation whatever to the fact that we just happen to be "polling" port number 255. (Can't help that the coincidence might be confusing.) If code 255 is read, execution branches to line 5Ø. If not, it defaults to line 4Ø. Execution returns to Line 1Ø where we begin the "polling" of the port again.

Astute observers have probably noted that we get either a 255, which apparently means DATA IS FLOWING, or a 127, which means it isn't. Why these particular numbers appear is beyond the scope of this book. The point is, DATA either IS or ISN'T flowing, and this is what INP reads, and acts upon.

If you want to have a little fun, Play the tape again but adjust the volume control very carefully (down around 2) so that variations in data flow are sensed and appear as changes in the message on the screen. Doesn't take much imagination to go from this point to different kinds of visual displays.

One more view of INP. Enter this program, and RUN.

```
1Ø FOR N = Ø TO 255

2Ø PRINT N; INP(N),

3Ø NEXT N
```

This program scans all 256 ports and gives us their status. They all report "255" except port #255. It should say "127", which we now know means

NO DATA COMING FROM CASSETTE

OUT

Let's see what OUT does. Remove any cassette from the recorder, and leave the hatch open so you can see the drive hub. Press the PLAY key, and type in this program:

```
1Ø INPUT"4 = ON    &   Ø = OFF";N

2Ø OUT 255,N

3Ø GOTO 1Ø
```

and RUN, responding to the INPut? and watching the drive hub.

We are sending directions OUT to port 255, the recorder port, and telling the motor to be either ON or OFF.

That's a sample of what OUT does. Nuff said.

Oh yes, the OUT in line 1Ø of the section on INP? Well, you see there's this little rubber band inside the Computer that has to be pulled to reset the . . .

VARPTR

While VARPTR is found in this version of BASIC, it's about as far from main-line BASIC as anything we have. It tells us where in memory a given variable is stored at a given time.

Enter this program:

```
1Ø  REM * VARPTR ADDRESS LOCATER *

2Ø  CLS

3Ø  FOR R = 1 TO 7 : READ A$(R)

4Ø  PRINT"THE CHARACTER IS  ";A$(R),

5Ø  PRINT"ITS ADDRESS IS  ",VARPTR(A$(R))

6Ø  PRINT : NEXT

7Ø  DATA A,B,C,D,1,2,3
```

       and RUN

The results are simple to understand. We "spun up" some DATA values in a string array, then let VARPTR tell us the addresses where those values were stored. Anything beyond that deals with assembly language, so we will only doff our hat in passing.

CHAPTER 23

The Expansion Interface

The TRS-80 can be connected directly to one Cassette Recorder and one additional device such as the Radio Shack Screen Printer. To use additional devices it becomes necessary to connect a "Black Box" that provides additional INPUT/OUTPUT jacks and can "talk" to each device. The TRS-80 Expansion Interface is such a box. It incorporates circuit cards which generate the necessary control signals, and has INPUT/OUTPUT jacks to operate up to four mini floppy drives, one printer, and two cassette recorders.

The Expansion Interface also has a digital clock circuit that can be read either by a machine language program (available free from Radio Shack) or the TRS-80 Disk Operating System (TRSDOS). Space is provided within the unit to install an additional circuit card to meet other specialized needs such as interfacing with RS-232 devices. Its most common use however is as a place to add an additional 16K or 32K bytes of memory, which adds to the 16K already inside the main computer case.

Setting It Up

Remove the Expansion Interface from its carton along with the ribbon cable, power supply, instruction book and other goodies. Some units are supplied with a buffer (a plastic box with ribbon cable attached at both ends) which is easily damaged if not handled carefully, or an extra DIN plug/jack assembly for connection between the Interface and the Computer.

Installing The Power Supplies

Remove the power supply compartment cover (located on the top right hand side of the Interface as you face it) by removing the three Phillips-head screws. Connect one Power Supply cable's 5-pin DIN plug to the matching 5-pin DIN connector on the edge of the printed circuit board. Place this power supply inside the Expansion Interface, closest to the front.

Notice that space is provided in the Interface compartment for two power supplies. This enables you to place the Computer's power supply out of sight along with the one for the Interface. If you choose to place the Computer's power supply in this compartment, route its cables thru the door cutouts in back. Connect the DIN plug to the power jack on the Computer as usual. Replace the power supply cover door on the Expansion Interface, being careful not to damage the case by over-tightening the screws.

Positioning The Expansion Interface

Place the Expansion Interface behind the TRS-80 Computer with the identification plate facing the Computer. The following tasks must be accomplished before plugging in A.C. power cables from the Computer power supply, Expansion Interface power supply, and any accessories.

Lift the little door covering the Expansion Port Connector on the TRS-80's left rear panel and slide it slightly to the right — then lift it up and away from the Computer. (Be careful not to break the little tabs.) Attach one end of the Expansion Ribbon Cable to this Expansion Port. It is important that the ribbon cable extends downward, out the **bottom** of each edge connector.

Units supplied with the buffered cable have arrows on the Buffer Box indicating which connector to attach to the Computer and which to the Expansion Interface. With non-buffered cables you may use either end. Attach the curved door onto the Computer case. It should close, allowing the ribbon cable to feed out between it and case.

Finally, attach the Expansion Ribbon Cable connector to the Bus jack located to the left of the push-button power switch on front of the Expansion Interface.

Turning It On

After all connections have been made and double checked, plug the A.C. power plugs from the two power supplies, plus the Video Display unit into an A.C. outlet. If you spring for a 3-wire power strip with switch, pilot light and circuit breaker (about $20), you will find it to be a great convenience and well worth the money. Turn on the Video Display unit, Expansion Interface, and, while holding down the BREAK key, turn on the TRS-80 Computer.

If MEMORY SIZE? is not displayed on the video monitor, turn off the Interface. Power up the Computer first, then turn on the Interface. The MEMORY SIZE? question should appear and you can respond to it as usual.

Another Gimmick

If you are not interested in using dual cassettes because you have no need for data storage, or you are using the Disk system, you can still make use of the cassette switching relay in the Expansion Interface as a noise generator for special effects. (Most expensive New Year's Eve noise maker in the house!)

Each time the Computer switches from cassette #1 to cassette #2 and back again, you'll hear a clicking sound. By increasing the switching speed, the slight click-sound becomes a buzz easily heard by all. Using the relay in this manner is not recommended if you intend to use the dual cassette feature in the future because you are reducing the life expectancy of the relay. Think of it as opening and closing your car door several hundred times each time you get in the car. Before long, either the door hinges or your arm will fail. (More probably the smog devices!)

Now that you know the pitfalls, try this program to hear the "buzzer" in action. Before RUNning, be certain both Recorders are disconnected from the Interface, to prevent possible damage to them, or a possible fusing together of the relay contacts.

```
1Ø  REM BUZZER GENERATOR

2Ø  PRINT "PRESS'B' TO HEAR THE BUZZER"

3Ø  A$=INKEY$: IF A$= "B" GOTO 5Ø

4Ø  GOTO 3Ø

5Ø  FOR X= 1 TO 5Ø

6Ø  POKE 143Ø8,1

7Ø  POKE 143Ø8,Ø

8Ø  NEXT X

9Ø  FOR X= 1 TO 1ØØ: NEXT

1ØØ GOTO 3Ø
```

By setting bit Ø at address 143Ø8 to 1, and then to Ø in lines 6Ø and 7Ø, the relay in the Interface switches back and forth between Cassette #2 and Cassette #1 respectively. This sound can be "tuned" somewhat by changing the relay switching-time in line 5Ø to generate the special effects used in game programs like Pong, Submarine, etc. . . .

Figure 1 shows the additional hookup points to the Expansion Interface. Note that connection point #3 is used for hooking to Radio Shack's line printers. Smaller printers which can be hooked directly to the TRS-80 bus, are connected at point #2, which is a direct extension of the TRS-80 bus.

The DIN jacks in the back will be discussed in more detail in the chapter dealing with dual cassette operation. Point #8, front and center, is used to connect to the optional RS-232 interface board.

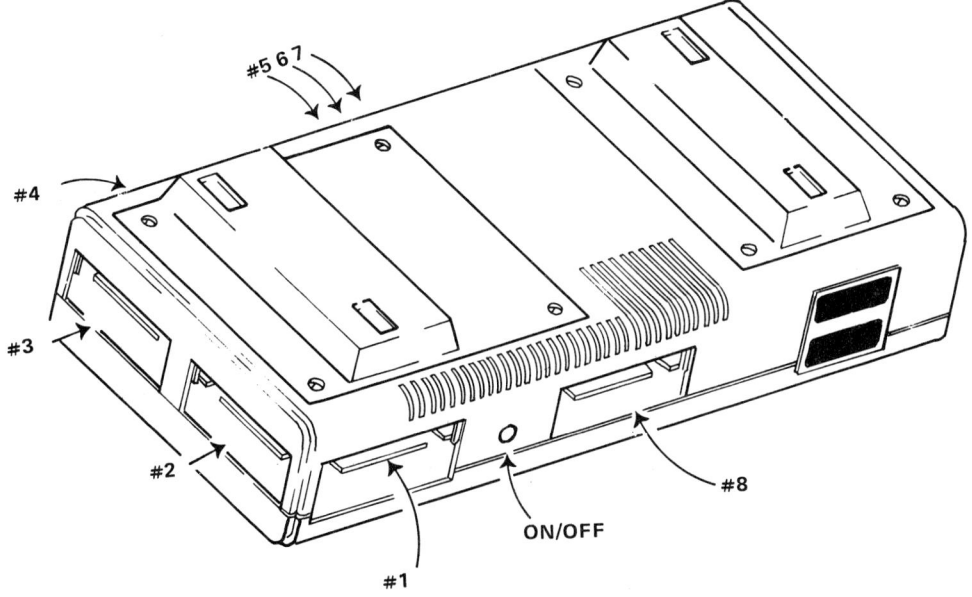

Use the utmost care in hooking up to these ports. Triple check to see that the right end of the cable is being used and that the cable always feeds **downward** from the connector. I've seen these interfaces and peripherals "buy the farm" when the user was experimenting with what should go where, and how — with the power ON. (No, it wasn't me . . . this time!)

LLIST and LPRINT

These BASIC Commands/Statements are almost too easy.

> LLIST is typed at the command level when you want a listing on the printer

> LPRINT is used in a program when you want the program to print something on the printer.

Both can be used either as statements or commands. If you want to print both on the screen and on paper, use duplicate program lines, with PRINT in the one for the screen, and LPRINT for the printer.

Enter any program of your choice and convert it to LPRINT the results on your printer. Make a "hard copy" LLISTing of it.

If you accidentally precede either PRINT or LIST with the letter L and don't have a printer connected, there may be trouble. It's especially easy to have a simple LIST turn into LLIST if the L key bounces. If an Expansion Interface is **not** connected, a simple RESET will make things OK again.

If an Interface **IS** connected, it automatically assumes (right or wrong) that Disk drives are also connected and won't let you do a simple RESET. You either have to hook up a printer and let it accept the information directed its way by the LLIST or LPRINT, or press RESET (with the BREAK key down), *losing your program in the process.*

If you have an Interface, you should do frequent dumps to cassette tape when developing new programs — **just in case.**

LPRINT TAB

We can only TAB as far as position 63 using LPRINT. To go beyond that point it is necessary to resort to devious means.

We can recall that PRINT STRING$ is used to repeat a number of characters or actions. We can use it to sneak around the above rule by having it repeat a number of spaces. For example:

```
1Ø LPRINT STRING$(75,32);X
```

will "print" 75 blank spaces before printing the value of X. "32" is the ASCII code for a blank space.

Advanced LPRINT Capabilities

5 different ASCII codes are set aside for use with printers. Since different printers respond differently, we can only talk here in general terms, and learn how to test our own printer to see how it responds. The 5 codes are:

1Ø	line feed and carriage return
11	roll paper to top of next sheet
12	roll paper to top of next sheet
13	line feed and carriage return
138	carriage return and line feed

To see what this all means, hook up your printer (assuming you have one . . . if not, guess you can stay with us and read on). Then enter this program:

```
1 CLS:PRINT

1Ø INPUT "ENTER A CODE NUMBER";N

2Ø LPRINT CHR$(N)

9Ø PRINT : LIST

        and RUN
```

Try each of the codes and see what happens. Some codes may do nothing. Your printer's manual may have additional (or replacement) codes.

There are no universal rules. Keep your test program simple and be aware that LPRINT with CHR$ is not always predictable when mixed on the same program line.

The "top of form" or "top of next sheet" feature is a necessary one for using the printer to prepare printed statements, or printing information which must always start at the top of a page. Users with "continuous roll" printers have little need for a "top of form".

When your Computer is turned on, if it's going to do any printing, it automatically assumes it will be printing 6 lines per inch on sheets of paper 11 inches long, 66 lines per page. This information is stored in memory location 16424. Type:

```
>PRINT PEEK (16424)
```

and we should get back the number

67

That's one more than the number of lines to be printed.

If we use a different size paper, we can change the number of lines for that page by POKEing in a different number. Suppose we are printing on paper that is 8 inches long. 8 inches times 6 lines per inch = 48. 48 + 1 = 49. We will:

```
>POKE 16424,49
```

In order for the "top of page" feature to work, it is also necessary for the Computer to keep track of how many lines have been printed on each page. This information is stored in memory location 16425. Let's PEEK:

```
>PRINT PEEK (16425)
```

and we'll get a number, the size of which depends on how many lines have already been printed. That will vary with how much experimenting we've been doing, and with which code.

The difference between how many lines **can** be printed on a page (memory location 16424) and how many **have** been printed (memory location 16425) tells the Computer how many have yet to be printed before starting the top of a new page. It's all very simple, in principle.

We can even POKE a 1 into location 16425 at the beginning of our program to initialize the counter. Each time we use a "form feed" code (11 or 12), the counter is reset back to 1 for a new page.

With a little experimenting, you will have your big printer doing what you paid to have it do.

Time Out

The Real Time Clock

The Expansion Interface has one additional feature — a Real Time clock. "Real Time" means "now" time. It contains a real clock, the time being controlled by an internal quartz crystal. In addition, that clock can be accessed (gotten to) by software (programs) and used to serve as an event-timer or master clock to control events. Up till now we've used simple FOR-NEXT loops to approximate times — satisfactory only over a short period.

The Level II ROM does not have the software built in to activate and control the clock. In order to use it, we must load in a machine language program from a tape furnished free by Radio Shack. That tape also includes the keyboard "debounce" program which we learned to load in the SYSTEM Chapter.

POKEing The Big Machine

Tighten your belt and put on the helmet. We are going to RAM the line — with finesse.

Power up the Computer and Expansion Interface. Since this entire book is about Level II, what follows does not apply to the Interface when used with floppy disks. The disk system has its own debounce routine which is activated automatically, as well as a clock routine that can be activated without going thru what we are about to do.

When the Computer asks

MEMORY SIZE_

Answer with:

65400 if you have 48K of RAM

49016 if you have 32K of RAM

32632 if you have 16K of RAM

20344 if you have 4K of RAM

> to leave room at the "top" of memory for both the keybounce and clock routines. (Users with either 4 or 16K of RAM would obviously be using the Interface box for other than to hold extra memory . . . there might be some of them, somewhere.)

The screen will verify we are in Level II BASIC and say

READY

>

We enter the SYSTEM mode by typing

SYSTEM

> and following the

*?   we type

RELO

> the name of the machine language program we want to read from Radio Shack's tape.

Set up the recorder to play the KEYBOARD DEBOUNCE/ REAL TIME CLOCK SYSTEM * RELO tape

> and press

ENTER

After a time, the usual asterisks will appear in the upper right hand corner, followed by another

*?   to which we respond

/ **ENTER**

The Computer wishes to engage us in rather extensive dialogue, saying:

```
TRS-80 RELOCATING LOADER
BASE  = (a hexidecimal number)
+
```

Ignoring it all, we charge blindly onward, and confidently press the single letter

S   and watch the screen. The recorder rolls, and up
         comes

```
KB DEBOUNCE ROUTINE.
```

         plus another

+   to which we say

L   (Doesn't really matter for now what all this
         means. That's for another time, place, and spe-
         cialized book. There are some hints as we go
         along, but not enough to divert us from the
         main thing we're trying to learn right now.)

Persistent, it is, and it chatters

```
LOCATING RELOCATION DIRECTORY.
LOADING RELOCATABLE CODE.
RELOCATION COMPLETE, BASE = (another HEX number)
```

This time we have to write down that HEX number since we will need to use it very soon. (If you have 32K of RAM you should get the number BFC8.) Again we see a

+   and with equal persistence we say again

S   (meaning Search for the next machine language program)

It says "I found it, and its name is"

    REAL TIME CLOCK
    +

Again we say "don't just sit there using up juice, LOAD it" and type an

    L

It repeats itself in a computerlike monotone, saying:

    LOADING RELOCATION DIRECTORY.
    LOADING RELOCATABLE CODE.
    RELOATION COMPLETE, BASE = (another HEX number)

Yes, we have to write this HEX number down, too. Don't get the two mixed up! (32K RAM users should get BF7A.) Seeing another

    +

we decide we've had enough of this chatter, and elect to Escape to BASIC by typing

    E   and see the welcome

    READY
    >

Whew! Another close scrape with machine language!

But there is more work to be done. We have to **activate** the KEYBOARD DEBOUNCE routine.

Turning to our HEX number notes, we look up the BASE of the DEBOUNCE routine. What do you have? 32K users got BFC8. Going to the HEX-to-Decimal conversion chart on the next page, we convert BFC8 to a decimal number. If you've forgotten how, follow me through this example:

Working from left to right:

B = 45056

F = 3840

C =   192   Add them all together and they spell

8 =   8
———————
     49096

HEX CODE	Most Significant Bytes		Least Significant Bytes	
	IV	III	II	I
Ø	Ø	Ø	Ø	Ø
1	4Ø96	256	16	1
2	8192	512	32	2
3	12288	768	48	3
4	16384	1Ø24	64	4
5	2Ø48Ø	128Ø	8Ø	5
6	24576	1536	96	6
7	28672	1792	112	7
8	32768	2Ø48	128	8
9	36864	23Ø4	144	9
A	4Ø96Ø	256Ø	16Ø	1Ø
B	45Ø56	2816	176	11
C	49152	3Ø72	192	12
D	53348	3328	2Ø8	13
E	57344	3584	224	14
F	6144Ø	384Ø	24Ø	15

Hex-to-Decimal Conversion Chart

Decimal Value = IV + III + II + I

Now, if you don't see how we got that, STOP right now and don't go on until you figure it out. We can't continue without knowing how to make these conversions. Go back to the SYSTEM chapter and review it there if necessary.

OK, the BASE of the KEYBOARD BOUNCE routine is at memory location 49096. We have to increase that number by one, then go back into machine language to activate the program.

Living with real gusto, we leap at the keyboard and type

SYSTEM

followed by

*? /49097

then flee to the safety of

READY
>

Closing in one the REAL TIME CLOCK, it's sweaty brow all the way. No way to avoid this machine language biz.

Look at the **second** HEX number you wrote down. It is the BASE of the CLOCK routine, and we must increase it by one, then get tricky. What number did you get? 32K users got BF7A. One number larger than BF7A must be BF7B. Look at the chart, if necessary.

Having made that startling discovery, we now have to split our HEX number into 2 parts — the *most* important, and the *least* important. (You know, things like this could easily give computers a bad reputation as being unnecessarily complex!)

Anyway, since the little numbers are always on the right, we say

7A represents the *least* significant bytes
        and, by uncanny reasoning, we conclude
BF must represent the *most* significant bytes

Now we get to convert them separately to decimal. Sticking with our 32K RAM example (you do your own thing if you have 4K, 16K or 48K of RAM — the example here illustrates the principle):

lsb = 7B = 112 + 11 = 123 decimal

msb = BF = 176 + 15 = 191 decimal

Terrific! What are we supposed to do with that? The fastest way to the answer is to type in this program, study it carefully, then RUN it.

```
1Ø REM * REAL TIME CLOCK PROGRAM *
2Ø CLS : PRINT "WE HAVE TO START BY
              SETTING THE CLOCK" : PRINT
3Ø INPUT"WHAT IS THE HOUR ";H
4Ø INPUT"WHAT ARE THE MINUTES ";M
5Ø INPUT"WHAT ARE THE SECONDS ";S : CLS
1ØØ POKE 16481, H          ' POKES IN THE
                            STARTING HOUR
11Ø POKE 1648Ø,M           ' POKES IN THE
                            STARTING MINUTES
12Ø POKE 16479,S           ' POKES IN THE
                            STARTING SECONDS
15Ø POKE 16526,123         ' SETS UP LSB FOR
                            A CALL FROM USR
16Ø POKE 16527,191         ' SETS UP MSB FOR
                            A CALL FROM USR
2ØØ X = USR(1)             'USR(1) STARTS CLOCK.
                                 USR(Ø) STOPS
3ØØ PRINT@5,"HOURS","MINUTES","SECONDS"
5ØØ PRINT@7Ø, PEEK(16481),PEEK(1648Ø),
                     PEEK(16479)
9999 GOTO 5ØØ
```

Pretty slick, eh? It's a minimum sort of program, but its expansion is limited only by your own imagination. As a starter, let's change line 5ØØ and add 51Ø:

```
5ØØ H=PEEK(16481) : M=PEEK(1648Ø)
                  : S=PEEK(16479)
51Ø PRINT@7Ø, H,M,S
```

        and RUN.

The modified program assigns variables to the hour, minute and second, giving us a means to compare them against other numbers. Add these lines:

```
6ØØ REM * USE OF LOGIC WITH REAL TIME CLOCK *
61Ø IF H = 12 AND M = 35 AND S = 52 THEN 1ØØØ
7ØØ GOTO5ØØ
1ØØØ REM * A ROUTINE NEEDED HERE TO
            THROW THE BIG SWITCH *
1Ø1Ø PRINT "HYDROTURBINE #7 STARTUP
            SEQUENCE INITIATED"
```

        and RUN.

Combining real time with program logic presents possibilities that boggle the mind. (To learn how to actually "throw the big switch" see *Controlling The World With Your TRS-80*. It is an entire book dedicated to designing, constructing and controlling hardware with BASIC software, and is made to order for those interested in this sort of thing. Published by CompuSoft. Same author. Ahem.)

RUN again, with this change:

```
1Ø1Ø PRINT@45Ø, "HYDROTURBINE #7 STARTUP
            SEQUENCE INITIATED"
```

But there's more! Add these lines:

```
2000 REM * LOGS ACTIVITIES ON CASSETTE TAPE *
2010 T = T + 1 : IF T =>2 GOTO 500
              'ONLY ONE WRITE TO TAPE
2020 X = USR(0)              ' SHUTS OFF CLOCK
2030 C = 71                  ' LET CODE 71
                 MEAN TURBINE 7 STARTUP
2040 PRINT #-1,C,H,M,S      ' LOG EVENT
                    AND TIME ON TAPE
2050 PRINT#648, "EVENT LOGGED ON TAPE"
2060 X = USR(1)              ' TURN CLOCK
                              BACK ON
```

and RUN.

Wow! Now we can maintain a log on tape of every event that occurs at the old powerhouse. It will be no problem at all to write a little program to INPUT that DATA back off tape and print on the screen or a printer.

You're wondering what lines 2020 and 2060 are all about? Well, the Real Time Clock, both in Disk and non-Disk systems, really screws up cassette operation. It's a technical problem which will hopefully be solved in future models. The clock **must** be turned off in order to do tape INPUTs and SAVEs. Don't try to CSAVE a program without first shutting off the clock (otherwise it won't take). Fortunately, the clock **can** be readily turned OFF and ON, both with program statements and at a command level by using

```
X=USR(0)
```

to turn it off

```
X=USR(1)
```

to turn it back on

In the process, some time is lost, and the clock will fall behind a bit. If every second is really that precious in your application, you could note that we lose about 5 seconds each time we log an event on tape. Can you think of an easy way to add 5 seconds to the time after such logging? Sure you can.

On the brighter side, if program execution is STOPped with the STOP statement or the BREAK key, the clock keeps running even tho the time isn't displayed on the screen. Typing CONT will resume program execution and the clock will be right on time.

Since the clock does not reset to zero at the end of 12 hours, you might say it's a 24 hour clock. Since it doesn't reset at the end of 24 hours either, maybe it's more of an elapsed time clock. In any case, if you want these resets, they have to be accomplished in the program software — not a very difficult task.

The final Coupe de Grace (our French speaking readers like a little of that sort of thing. Wonder what it means?) for this Chapter is the automatic logging of events on your printer. If you don't have a printer yet, beware of line 112Ø, since execution freezes until a printer accepts that line. Just put a REM there if you don't have a printer.

```
11ØØ REM * LOGS ACTIVITIES ON PRINTER *

111Ø N = N + 1 : IF N => 2 GOTO 5ØØ
               ' PRINT ONLY ONCE

112Ø LPRINT"TURBINE #7 STARTUP
            BEGAN AT ";H;M;S

113Ø PRINT@584, "EVENT LOGGED ON PRINTER"
```

So, cock the recorder, turn on the printer, set the clock at a little before 12:35:52, and stand aside.

49 . . . 5Ø . . .51 . . . 52 KERCHUNK!!! There goes the big turbine . . . it's starting to wind up! Ratatatatata, the printer is getting it all down. Hmmmmmm Hmmmmm Hmmmmmm, round and round go the tape hubs. Yep . . . the video screen is reporting the action.

RUN it again, Sam . . . RUN it again! (as Wagner's euphoric "Ride of the Valkerie" swirls in our head).

Breathes there a man with soul so dead, who never to himself has said . . .

"This must be how good the old sow feels wallowing in wet mud on a hot day."

MUSIC: Up and out.

NOTES

CHAPTER 25

Dual Cassette Operation

With the Expansion Interface's dual cassette feature, it is possible to Read and Write data from and to tape using two separate and independent cassette recorders. A similar feat can now be performed using one recorder and two cassette tapes, but it can be tedious to the point of being impractical. Two recorders, one set to PLAY and the other to RECORD, provides a practical, reliable and economical way of using your TRS-80 to perform genuine "Data Processing."

Setting Up For Dual Cassettes

Connect the Tape Interconnection Cable (the one with a 5-pin DIN plug on each end) from the Computer's TAPE jack to the Expansion Interface cassette INPUT/OUTPUT connector (the DIN connector located on the back panel **next to the power cables** — Point #6). Connect the DIN plug from a Cassette Recorder (designated as #1) to the DIN jack on the Interface's back panel located **next to the Mini Disk port** — Point #4. The other end of this cable should be connected to the Cassette Recorder as you would for single recorder operation.

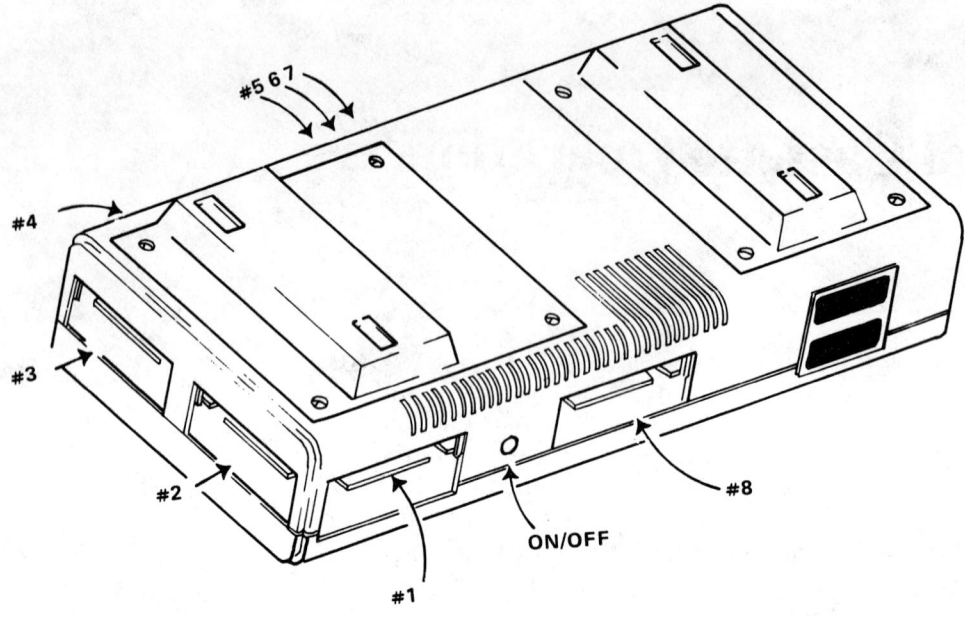

Connect the cable from the second Cassette Recorder (designated #2) to the remaining DIN jack on the Interface back panel. (The **center** DIN jack, point #5.)

Now that the dual cassette connectors on the Expansion Interface have been identified, attach stick-on labels to the back of the Interface case (above each connector) to save time trying to identify them again in the future.

Enter this program to verify that the two Recorders are connected properly and are ready for use. Position the recorders with the access doors open so you can see the drive spindles. It helps to leave the cassettes out at this time. Press the PLAY key on each, and RUN.

```
1Ø REM * DUAL CASSETTE TEST *

2Ø CLS : PRINT "TYPE '1' TO RUN CASSETTE #1"

3Ø PRINT "TYPE '2' TO RUN CASSETTE #2"

4Ø N$ = INKEY$ : IF N$ = "" GOTO 4Ø

5Ø IF VAL(N$) = 1 THEN PRINT#-1,1

6Ø IF VAL(N$) = 2 THEN PRINT#-2,1

7Ø GOTO 4Ø
```

Alternate between pressing the "1" key and "2" key. Watch the drive spindles on both Recorders to see that each is operating as we have instructed. If you use CTR-80's, watch for the red light as well.

When using the Interface, the recorders can be addressed individually. Number 1 is identified as #-1 and number 2 is #−2. Any combination of both on PLAY, both on RECORD, one doing each or both doing neither can be used.

When CLOADing and CSAVing, if neither recorder is specified, #1 is automatically assumed. The correct way to specify each is:

```
CSAVE#-1,"A"          or      CSAVE#-2,"A"
```

and

```
CLOAD#-1,"A"          or      CLOAD#-2,"A"
```

To check for a good load, use either

CLOAD#-1?"A"   or   CLOAD#-2, ?"A"

CLOAD? by itself with automatically default to test for a good load on the first program encountered on drive #1.

You will recall back in the Level I manual we had a program for logging Temperature and Humidity, and in Part I of this book an upgraded version was shown. We're going to use that upgrade now — first to refresh our memory on how to use a single cassette, then modifying it to use twin cassettes.

The program is reprinted here for your convenience. If you saved it on tape before, CLOAD it in. If not, start typing.

```
10 REM   * TEMPERATURE AND HUMIDITY RECORDING PROGRAM *
20 REM   * DATA STORAGE MUST START ON THE 1ST DAY OF MONTH *
40 CLS : INPUT"WHAT DAY OF THE MONTH IS IT";D
50 INPUT"WHAT IS TODAYS TEMPERATURE"; T
60 INPUT"WHAT IS TODAYS HUMIDITY"; H
70 PRINT:PRINT
80 IF D = 1 GOTO 430          ' ON FIRST DAY IS NO PRIOR DATA
100 REM   * INPUTTING DATA STORED ON CASSETTE TAPE *
110 PRINT"WE MUST LOAD PRIOR DAYS TEMP & HUMIDITY FROM"
120 PRINT"THE DATA TAPE. BE SURE IT'S REWOUND AND THE RECORDER"
130 PRINT"IS SET TO 'PLAY'. " : PRINT : PRINT
140 INPUT"PRESS 'ENTER' WHEN EVERYTHING IS READY TO GO. "; A$
160 CLS:PRINT"DATA IS NOW FLOWING INTO THE COMPUTER FROM TAPE. "
170 PRINT : PRINT : PRINT"DATE", "TEMP", "HUMIDITY" : PRINT
180 FOR X = 1 TO D-1
190 INPUT #-1, Y, Z              ' BRINGS IT IN FROM TAPE
195 PRINT X, Y, Z                ' PRINTS IT ON THE SCREEN
200 B = B+Y : C = C+Z            ' KEEPS RUNNING TOTALS
210 NEXT X
300 REM   * MONTHS AVERAGES TO-DATE *
310 B = (B+T)/D : C = (C+H)/D    ' COMPUTES THE AVERAGES
320 PRINT D, T, H
330 PRINT : PRINT "   **    THIS MONTHS AVERAGES   **"
340 PRINTTAB(7); "TEMP"; TAB(17); "HUMIDITY"
350 PRINTTAB(7); B; TAB(19); C
400 REM   * STORING TODAYS TEMP & HUMIDITY ON TAPE *
410 PRINT:PRINT:INPUT"PRESS 'ENTER' WHEN READY TO CONTINUE"; A$
420 CLS : PRINT : PRINT
430 PRINT"TODAYS TEMPERATURE AND HUMIDITY WILL NOW BE PRINTED"
440 PRINT"ON THE DATA TAPE. BE SURE 'RECORD' & 'PLAY' ARE"
450 PRINT"PRESSED. DO NOT REWIND THE TAPE, YET. " : PRINT
460 INPUT"WHEN ALL IS READY, PRESS 'ENTER'"; A$ : CLS
470 PRINT"TODAYS DATA IS NOW FLOWING FROM THE COMPUTER TO THE"
480 PRINT"TAPE. WE WILL INPUT THIS PLUS THE EARLIER DATA "
490 PRINT"TOMORROW. " : PRINT
500 PRINT #-1, T, H               ' PRINTS TODAY ON TAPE
520 PRINT"TODAYS NUMBERS HAVE BEEN ADDED TO THE TAPE. "
530 PRINT"REWIND THE TAPE IN PREPARATION FOR TOMORROW. "
```

RUN the program through several days of arbitrary temperatures and humidity — enough to make a DATA tape.

Now let's modify the program and have cassette #1 act as the source of our historical DATA, and cassette #2 the place we will record the updated DATA. This means we will INPUT from #1 and PRINT to #2.

Fire up the Editor and make the program read like this:

```
10 REM  * TEMP AND HUMIDITY RECORDING PROGRAM USING 2 TAPES *
20 REM  * DATA STORAGE MUST START ON THE 1ST DAY OF MONTH *
40 CLS : INPUT"WHAT DAY OF THE MONTH IS IT";D
50 INPUT"WHAT IS TODAYS TEMPERATURE";T
60 INPUT"WHAT IS TODAYS HUMIDITY";H
70 PRINT:PRINT
80 IF D = 1 GOTO 430            ' ON FIRST DAY IS NO PRIOR DATA
100 REM  * INPUTTING DATA STORED ON CASSETTE TAPE *
110 PRINT"WE MUST LOAD PRIOR DAYS TEMP & HUMIDITY FROM"
120 PRINT"TAPE DRIVE #1. BE SURE THE LATEST TAPE IS REWOUND"
130 PRINT"AND THE RECORDER IS SET TO 'PLAY'. " : PRINT
140 PRINT"PUT FRESH TAPE IN DRIVE #2, AND SET TO RECORD. "
150 PRINT:INPUT"PRESS 'ENTER' WHEN BOTH TAPES ARE READY. ";A$
160 CLS:PRINT"DATA IS NOW FLOWING FROM DRIVE #1 INTO THE"
165 PRINT"COMPUTER, AND FROM THERE BEING RE-RECORDED ON #2"
170 PRINT : PRINT : PRINT"DATE", "TEMP", "HUMIDITY" : PRINT
180 FOR X = 1 TO D-1
190 INPUT #-1, Y, Z             ' BRINGS IT IN FROM TAPE ,
195 PRINT X, Y, Z               ' PRINTS IT ON THE SCREEN
197 PRINT #-2, Y, Z             ' PRINTS IT ON DRIVE #2
200 B = B+Y : C = C+Z           ' KEEPS RUNNING TOTALS
210 NEXT X
300 REM  * MONTHS AVERAGES TO-DATE *
310 B = (B+T)/D : C = (C+H)/D   ' COMPUTES THE AVERAGES
320 PRINT D, T, H
330 PRINT : PRINT "   **   THIS MONTHS AVERAGES  **"
340 PRINTTAB(7); "TEMP"; TAB(17); "HUMIDITY"
350 PRINTTAB(7); B; TAB(19); C : PRINT : GOTO 470
430 PRINT"BE SURE THERE IS A FRESH TAPE IN DRIVE #2 AND"
440 INPUT"IT IS SET TO RECORD. PRESS 'ENTER' WHEN READY";A$
470 PRINT"TODAYS DATA NOW FLOWING FROM COMPUTER TO DRIVE #2. "
480 PRINT"WE WILL INPUT THIS PLUS THE EARLIER DATA FROM DRIVE"
490 PRINT"#2, TOMORROW. " : PRINT
500 PRINT #-2, T, H             ' PRINTS TODAY ON TAPE #2
525 PRINT"RECORDING COMPLETE. " : PRINT
530 PRINT"REWIND & STORE TAPE #2 IN PREPARATION FOR TOMORROW. "
540 PRINT"KEEP THE OLD TAPE AS A BACKUP FOR AT LEAST ONE DAY. "
```

RUN the modified program through at least 5 days temperature and humidity readings to get a good feel for how it works.

Pretty nifty, huh!

This learning program is not an ideal model of programming technique for dual cassette operation. It was written to cause lots of relay clicking, turning on and off of motors, blinking lights and screen action, and help us LEARN what's going on. It contains far more explanatory verbage than actual program logic.

Due to the chance of an error everytime a relay is switched, or motor started or stopped, in actual practice it's best to keep the mechanical action to a minimum. How can we do this?

Make the data dumps, both to and from the Computer, as large as possible each time a motor is actuated. Ideally, we might have only one dump from drive #1 to the Computer at the beginning of a session; then only one dump from the Computer to drive #2 at the end. The software and Computer reliability are exceedingly high. Enhance the software as much as possible to cut down on reliance on hardware. Got any ideas?

How about this one? Could we set up an array that is 31 days long by 2 pieces of data wide? Yes.

Could we then dump to tape the entire array, with all addresses initialized to zero? Yes.

Could we then bring in this "null array" in one tape-read, change the data for only one day, then unload the entire array in one dump? Yes. Could we even improve on this idea? Yes.

There you have it! Users who are serious about data processing with cassette tape have their assignment.

Precautions

Those who are serious about using ordinary cassette tape recorders for computer work should bear in mind that they were designed for recording talk and music, not digital data. We are only using them because they are inexpensive and available.

Only the very highest quality tape should be used. Certified tape, such as that sold at Radio Shack stores is a bit expensive — but required if you want high reliability. Quality is even more critical in DATA applications than for storing programs. We normally make only one recording of the DATA instead of multiple dumps, and only one READ, tho that could be changed in the software.

Periodic maintenance is a must. Tape heads must be cleaned after every few hours use, and demagnetized frequently. The tape drives and tapes must be kept impeccably clean. Data Processing is not the same as just "fooling around" with computers, and erratic tape systems will drive you to drink faster than any software bug. (Hic!).

If approached with purposeful diligence and an understanding of the level of technology we are dealing with, cassette systems can do the job.

POSTLUDE

From the Promotory

Well, we've come a long way. It's time to pull up the old wagon train, scan the horizon and see where we are.

We've hacked our way through the jungles of Level I and converting it to Level II. We've forged the swamps of Strings and portaged across machine language without getting too wet. Having mastered most of BASIC, we stand now at the threshold of the next frontier — disk systems.

Many readers will branch off on the long trail, seeking to control hardware with their TRS-80 before going to disk. Others will head over the pass directly to disk. Most will wonder if they can ever master the complexities. I wish you well in your journeys, and, if you wish, I'll be there waiting to help you through.

Have a good trip!

"Appendix"

"WELL, YOUR APPENDIX IS SOMEWHAT ENLARGED, BUT WE'VE DECIDED TO LEAVE IT IN..."

"SCIENCE LEARNS MOST FROM ITS ERRORS!"

Appendix A

LEVEL II Error Message
Reference Guide

?BS is displayed by the Computer when the elements in a numeric or string matrix are beyond the range of values reserved in the DIM statement.

BS (Subscript out of Range) Code 9

TEST PROGRAM

```
1Ø REM 'BS' ERROR MESSAGE GENERATOR

2Ø PRINT "THE VALUE OF X IS";

3Ø A(X)=1

4Ø PRINT X;

5Ø X=X+1

6Ø GOTO 3Ø
```

SAMPLE RUN

```
THE VALUE OF X IS Ø 1 2 3 4 5 6 7 8 9 1Ø
?BS ERROR IN 3Ø
```

Matrix A(X) has not been formally dimensioned so the Computer automatically reserves space for 11 elements (Ø to 1Ø). The value of X is incremented by one in line 5Ø and when the value of X reaches 11 the matrix exceeds its reserved space. Its subscript is then out of range.

The DIM value can be varied depending on the number of Matrix elements needed and the available memory space.

By redimensioning the array, more elements can be stored. Adding this line expands the maximum matrix size to 4Ø elements.

```
25 DIM A(4Ø)
```

?CN is displayed when the command CONT or CONTINUE (either one works) is typed and there is no program to continue, the program has just been EDITed, or a line has just been added or deleted. CONT was originally designed to cause execution to resume after hitting a STOP, without initializing the variables to zero. In this interpreter, it can be used instead of RUN without a prior STOP.

**CN (Can't Continue)
Code 17**

To generate this error message, type NEW **ENTER** then CONT **ENTER** . Since we removed all programs it can't CONTINUE and displays the error message:

    ?CN ERROR

Another cause of the message is typing

    CONT ###

        when that line number doesn't exist.

?DD is displayed when the Computer is told to DIMension a numeric or string Matrix after it has already been DIMensioned earlier in the same program. It is protesting "Double Dimensioning."

DD (Redimensioned Array)
Code 10

TEST PROGRAM

```
1Ø REM 'DD' ERROR MESSAGE GENERATOR

2Ø DIM A(2Ø)

3Ø INPUT "ENTER A VALUE FOR MATRIX A(15)";A(15)

4Ø PRINT "THE VALUE OF MATRIX A(15) IS";A(15)

5Ø GOTO 2Ø
```

SAMPLE RUN

```
ENTER A VALUE FOR MATRIX A(15)? 5
THE VALUE OF MATRIX A(15) IS 5
? DD ERROR IN 2Ø
```

An attempt was made in line 5Ø to redimension A.

To see this program run error free, change line 5Ø to GOTO 3Ø and RUN. The Computer sees the DIM statement for array A only once.

?/∅ is displayed when the Computer is asked to divide a number by ∅. You may think of your Computer as the smartest thing going, but it is not capable of handling numbers of infinite value.

At the command level type:

PRINT 4/∅

The Computer responds with

?/∅ ERROR

/∅ (Division by Zero)
Code 11

The same error occurs when a program calls for division using a variable that has either been initialized to ∅ or has never been assigned a value larger than ∅. (All variables are initially set to zero when RUN is typed.) Here is a typical example of how the error may occur in a program:

TEST PROGRAM

```
1∅ REM /∅ ERROR MESSAGE GENERATOR

2∅ N=2∅

3∅ X=1∅

4∅ PRINT N;"DIVIDED BY";X;"EQUALS";N/X

5∅ PRINT N;"DIVIDED BY";Y;"EQUALS";N/Y
```

SAMPLE RUN

```
2∅ DIVIDED BY 1∅ EQUALS 2

2∅ DIVIDED BY ∅ EQUALS

?/∅ ERROR IN 5∅
```

The Computer does fine until it reaches line 5∅ and is asked to divide the value of variable N by a variable (Y) that has not been assigned a value other than zero.

?FC is displayed when illegal values are used with the built-in math functions or the Computer cannot figure out what to compute because of the values it received.

FC (Illegal Function Call)
Code 5

TEST PROGRAM #1

```
1Ø REM 'FC' ERROR MESSAGE GENERATOR
2Ø PRINT "TRY TO COMPUTE THE SQUARE ROOT OF -5"
3Ø PRINT SQR(-5)
```

SAMPLE RUN

```
TRY TO COMPUTE THE SQUARE ROOT OF -5
?FC ERROR IN 3Ø
```

The Computer is unable to compute the square root of a negative number in line 3Ø so it stops and displays the error message.

The same error message is displayed by substituting RND for SQR in line 3Ø because the Computer cannot produce a random value from a negative designation.

An FC error message is also displayed when a negative number is used in a DIM statement or a numeric or string array. Try RUNning each of the following:

```
1Ø DIM A(-5)
1Ø A(-5)=1Ø
1Ø INPUT A$(-5)
```

If you attempt to use the USR function and haven't boned up on machine language programming, you will no doubt see the FC error message displayed. When the Computer cannot find the starting address (must be POKED in by you) in which to run the machine language routine, it stops and displays the FC error message. To demonstrate this for yourself, type the command

```
PRINT USR(N)
```

Since we did not POKE in a starting address, the Computer responds with:

```
?FC ERROR
```

?FD is displayed when the Computer fails to read the proper data from cassette tape during the INPUT#-1 statement.

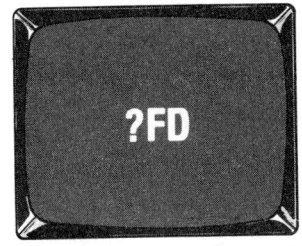

FD (Bad File Data)
Code 22

TEST PROGRAM

```
1Ø REM 'FD' ERROR MESSAGE GENERATOR
2Ø READ A$
3Ø PRINT A$
4Ø PRINT#-1,A$
5Ø IF A$="999"GOTO 7Ø
6Ø GOTO 2Ø
7Ø INPUT"REWIND, PRESS PLAY, THEN PRESS 'ENTER'";X$
8Ø INPUT#-1,A
9Ø PRINT A
1ØØ IF A=999 END
11Ø GOTO 8Ø
12Ø DATA A,B,999
```

SAMPLE RUN
```
A
B
999
REWIND, PRESS PLAY, THEN PRESS 'ENTER"?
```

Place a blank tape in the cassette recorder and set to the RECORD mode. RUN the program and follow the directions on the screen.

The program recorded string data on the tape in line 4Ø. Line 8Ø tried to read it back as numeric data. When the Computer recognized it was receiving bad data, it stopped and displayed
```
?FD ERROR IN 8Ø
```

To see this program run without the FD error, change the DATA in line 12Ø to all numbers
```
12Ø DATA 1,2,3,999
```

and RUN.

?ID is displayed when the Computer is asked to INPUT a value or string in the Immediate or Direct mode. The INPUT and INPUT#-1 statements can only be used in a program. Type each of these commands:

```
INPUT A

INPUT A$

INPUT#-1
```

Each is refused by the Computer, which displays

```
?ID ERROR
```

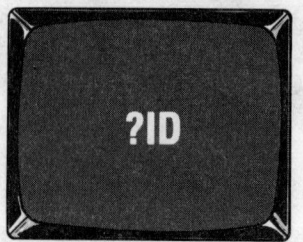

ID (Illegal Direct)
Code 12

?L3 is displayed by the Computer when a statement or command is used that is not part of Level II BASIC, but is part of TRS-80 Disk BASIC. Type the command:

PRINT TIME$

The Computer cannot find this function in its Level II interpreter but recognizes it as one of the Disk BASIC functions so it displays the error message:

?L3 ERROR

Try also

SAVE

and LOAD

L3 (Disk BASIC)
Code 23

?LS is displayed when an attempt is made to store more than 255 letters or characters in a string variable.

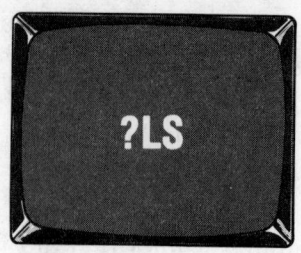

LS (String Too Long)
Code 15

TEST PROGRAM

```
1Ø REM 'LS' ERROR MESSAGE GENERATOR

2Ø CLEAR 1ØØØ

3Ø N$="X":N=1

4Ø N=N+N:PRINT N,

5Ø N$=N$+N$: PRINT N$

6Ø GOTO 4Ø
```

The CLEAR statement in line 2Ø reserves enough money space to allow it to hold up to a total of 1ØØØ string characters. The interpreter, however, does not permit any one string variable to hold more than 255 characters. When an attempt is made in line 5Ø to place 256 letters in variable N$, the Computer stops and displays the error message;

```
?LS ERROR IN 5Ø
```

Lines 3Ø-4Ø also provide a "counter" to show how many characters are assigned to N$ on each pass.

?MO is displayed when the Computer is not given all the information required to carry out its directive.

For example, type the command:

CSAVE

MO (Missing Operand)
Code 21

Since the program name was omitted from the CSAVE command, the Computer cannot execute it. It displays the error message:

?MO ERROR

To avoid this error, add a single letter or number program name to the CSAVE command, such as:

CSAVE"A"

?NF is displayed when an attempt is made to RUN a program containing a FOR-NEXT loop, but the word "FOR" is missing.

**NF (NEXT without FOR)
Code 1**

TEST PROGRAM #1

```
1Ø REM 'NF' ERROR GENERATOR

2Ø PRINT "WATCH OUT - - - HERE COMES THE NF ERROR"

3Ø NEXT
```

SAMPLE RUN

```
WATCH OUT - - - HERE COMES THE NF ERROR
?NF ERROR IN 3Ø
```

The Computer prints the message in line 2Ø, then looks back for an unused "FOR" statement.

The NF error is also displayed when the variable following a NEXT statement does not match the one following "FOR". Add these lines to the TEST program and RUN;

```
15 FOR X=1 TO 1Ø

3Ø NEXT Y
```

The "NEXT Y" in line 3Ø does not match the only FOR statement, in line 15.

The NF error message is also printed when nested FOR-NEXT loops are out of sequence. That is, one FOR-NEXT loop overlaps the other.

?NF

TEST PROGRAM #2

```
1Ø REM 'NF' ERROR IN A NESTED FOR-NEXT LOOP

2Ø FOR X=1 TO 2

3Ø   FOR Y=1 TO 4

4Ø    PRINT "NF ERROR COMING FROM FAULTY NESTED LOOPING"

5Ø NEXT X

6Ø   NEXT Y
```

SAMPLE RUN

```
NF ERROR COMING FROM FAULTY LOOPING
NF ERROR COMING FROM FAULTY LOOPING
?NF ERROR IN 6Ø
```

Line 4Ø is printed twice before the NF error message hits, since a NEXT statement cannot send the Computer back in the program beyond a FOR statement that has not found its match.

It's acceptable in Level II BASIC to omit the variable following the NEXT statement. The Computer loops back in the program and finds a FOR statement that complements the NEXT statement, thereby avoiding FOR-NEXT statements with variables out of sequence.

To demonstrate this feature, remove the variables X and Y from lines 5Ø and 6Ø in TEST PROGRAM #2 and RUN. The Computer searches out the appropriate FOR statement and prints line 4Ø eight times, without error.

?NR is displayed when an ON ERROR GOTO statement is used to branch to a specified program line, and the Computer does not encounter a RESUME statement before the program stops. The NR error message is not displayed if the END statement is used after the ERROR routine.

NR (No RESUME)
Code 18

TEST PROGRAM

```
1Ø REM 'NR' ERROR MESSAGE PROGRAM

2Ø ON ERROR GOTO 1ØØ

3Ø GOTO 5

1ØØ PRINT "AN ERROR SENT ME TO LINE 1ØØ"
```

SAMPLE RUN

```
AN ERROR SENT ME TO LINE 1ØØ

?NR ERROR IN 1ØØ
```

Not finding the line 5 specified in line 3Ø, the Computer displays the message in line 1ØØ. Since it does not find a RESUME statement, it stops and displays the NR error message. To prevent **this** error, add either of these statements.

```
11Ø END
```

or `11Ø RESUME`

and create some new problems.

?OD is displayed when the Computer is told to READ more items from the DATA statements than are available.

OD (Out of Data)
Code 4

TEST PROGRAM #1

```
1∅ REM 'OD' ERROR MESSAGE GENERATOR

2∅ FOR X=1 TO 5

3∅ READ A

4∅ PRINT A,

5∅ NEXT

6∅ DATA 9,8,7,6
```

SAMPLE RUN

```
?OD ERROR IN 3∅
```

Lines 2∅ through 5∅ enable the Computer to READ and PRINT numbers from the DATA statement five times. During the 5th pass of FOR-NEXT loop, however, the READ statement can't find a fifth piece of DATA. The program is literally "out of DATA".

An OD error message is also displayed when the INPUT#-1 statement asks for more DATA than is available on a cassette DATA tape.

?OD

TEST PROGRAM #2

```
1Ø REM 'OD' ERROR CAUSED BY MISSING TAPE DATA

2Ø READ A,B,C

3Ø PRINT A,B,C

4Ø PRINT#-1,A,B,C,

5Ø PRINT "REWIND TAPE, SET RECORDER TO PLAY,"

6Ø INPUT "THEN PRESS 'ENTER'";X$

7Ø INPUT#-1,A,B,C,D

8Ø PRINT A,B,C,D

9Ø DATA 1,2,3,4
```

Place a blank tape in the cassette recorder and set it to RECORD. Then RUN the program and follow instructions.

SAMPLE RUN

```
 2               2               3
REWIND TAPE, SET RECORDER TO PLAY,
THEN PRESS 'ENTER'?
?OD ERROR IN 7Ø
```

The Computer recorded 3 numbers on tape in line 4Ø but it is looking for 4 items in line 7Ø. Once the Computer senses it is missing one number, it stops the recorder and displays the error message.

?OM is displayed when an attempt is made to store a program larger than the Computer's memory storage space. It is also displayed when a matrix variable is assigned more elements than there is space in memory to store it.

For example, this program cannot run on a Computer with a memory size of 16K bytes or less.

OM (Out of Memory)
Code 7

TEST PROGRAM

```
1Ø REM 'OM'ERROR MESSAGE GENERATOR
2Ø DIM A(7Ø,7Ø)
3Ø FOR X=1 TO 5Ø
4Ø   FOR Y=1 TO 5Ø
5Ø     PRINT X,Y
6Ø   NEXT Y
7Ø NEXT X
```

SAMPLE RUN

```
?OM ERROR IN 1Ø
```

The Computer "saves" space in memory for matrix "A" with the DIM statement in line 2Ø. Change the values in line 2Ø to DIM A(5Ø,5Ø) and check remaining memory space by adding

```
25 PRINT MEM
```

This modified program can run error-free in machines with 16K bytes of memory, and have room to spare.

Another activity that eats up lots of memory space is to answer the MEMORY? question (asked when the Computer is turned on or is RESET) with a value that reserves too much memory for machine language or for the SYSTEM function. To generate this error, turn off your 16K Computer, let it settle down a few seconds, then turn it back on. Answer the MEMORY? question with the value 18ØØØ and check available memory with PRINT MEM. It would now be difficult to store a moderate sized BASIC program since we have reserved most of the memory space for other uses.

?OS is displayed when more letters or characters are assigned to a string variable than it is
capable of storing.

OS (Out of String Space)
Code 14

TEST PROGRAM

```
1Ø  REM 'OS'ERROR MESSAGE GENERATOR

2Ø  N$=N$+"A"

3Ø  N=N+1

4Ø  PRINT N;

5Ø  PRINT N$

6Ø  GOTO 2Ø
```

The letter "A" is added to the variable N$ until the Computer
runs out of space reserved for string variables. (5Ø bytes are
reserved on power-up.) It then stops and displays the error message:

```
?OS ERROR IN 3Ø
```

It is possible to increase or decrease the string storage space by
changing the space reserved for strings using the CLEAR statement. Type CLEAR 1Ø and RUN.

See how this reduces the number of characters that variable N$
can store? The sum of the spaces required for the last 2 values
of the string must be within the string space allocation. 5+4=9.

If CLEAR Ø is typed, all string space is removed, making it
impossible for string variables to store a single letter or character. Try it.

?OV is displayed when the Computer is unable to use a number because it is either too large or too small. An overflow condition can also be created by routine mathematical calculations at either the statement or command levels. Type

PRINT 25↑5Ø

(25 to the 5Øth power)

OV (Overflow)
Code 6

Being far beyond the Computer's maximum number handling capacity of 1.7Ø1411+E38, the OV message appears.

When arrived at by a program calculation the same thing happens:

TEST PROGRAM #1

```
1Ø REM 'OV' ERROR MESSAGE DUE TO STATEMENT

2Ø N = 1

3Ø PRINT 5Ø↑N,

4Ø N = N + 1

5Ø GOTO 3Ø
```

SAMPLE RUN

```
5Ø            25ØØ           125ØØ            6.25E+Ø6
```

etc.

```
?OV ERROR IN 3Ø
```

Another cause of overflow is attempting to store a number larger than is allowed (32767) in a variable designated as an integer (by the % operator).

?OV

TEST PROGRAM #2

```
10 REM 'OV' ERROR MESSAGE GENERATOR

20 PRINT "WATCH TNE NUMBER GROW"

30 A% = 32500

40 A% = A% + 1

50 PRINT @23,A%

60 GOTO 40
```

RUN this sample program and watch the number increase in value from 32500 to 32767. When the Computer is asked to add the value 1 to variable A% when it's storing the value 32767, it cannot comply since it is already at its maximum. The Computer stops and displays the error message:

```
?OV ERROR IN 40
```

?REDO is printed when a letter or string is typed where an INPUT statement calls for a number.

REDO (Type a number)
No Code Number

TEST PROGRAM

```
1Ø REM 'REDO' ERROR GENERATOR

2Ø INPUT "TYPE ANY NUMBER";N

3Ø PRINT N
```

SAMPLE RUN

```
TYPE ANY NUMBER? X
?REDO
TYPE ANY NUMBER?
```

After rejecting the letter X as not being a number, it returns execution to the INPUT line where the ERROR occurred, without crashing the program. Very handy indeed! And REDO is not one of the 23 "standard" error codes.

?RG is displayed when the Computer reads a RETURN statement and there is no corresponding GOSUB.

RG (RETURN without GOSUB)
Code 3

TEST PROGRAM #1

```
1Ø REM 'RG'ERROR MESSAGE GENERATOR

2Ø PRINT "AN EXAMPLE OF THE RG ERROR"

3Ø RETURN
```

SAMPLE RUN

```
AN EXAMPLE OF THE RG ERROR
?RG ERROR IN 3Ø
```

There is no GOSUB statement to match the RETURN in line 3Ø.

A common programming mistake made when using the GOSUB statement, is not providing protection against reading the same RETURN statement more than once. For example, enter this program in your Computer and RUN;

?RG

TEST PROGRAM #2

```
1Ø REM 'RG' ERROR MESSAGE GENERATOR

2Ø GOSUB 5Ø

3Ø PRINT "I HAVE RETURNED FROM THE SUBROUTINE"

4Ø PRINT "NOTHING HERE TO STOP ME"

5Ø PRINT "THIS IS A TYPICAL SUBROUTINE"

6Ø RETURN
```

SAMPLE RUN

```
THIS IS A TYPICAL SUBROUTINE
I HAVE RETURNED FROM THE SUBROUTINE
NOTHING HERE TO STOP ME
THIS IS A TYPICAL SUBROUTINE
?RG ERROR IN 6Ø
```

The RG error message is printed because there was no block protecting the RETURN statement in line 6Ø. To prevent this, change line 4Ø to

```
4Ø END
```

?RW is displayed when the Computer encounters a RESUME statement without first finding an ON ERROR GOTO statement.

**RW (RESUME without ERROR)
Code 19**

TEST PROGRAM

```
1Ø REM 'NR' ERROR MESSAGE PROGRAM

2Ø RESUME

3Ø ON ERROR GOTO 1ØØ

4Ø READ A

5Ø END

1ØØ PRINT "SEE THE ERROR IN LINE 4Ø?"
```

The Computer reads the RESUME statement in line 2Ø, but since it hasn't seen an ON ERROR GOTO statement yet, it stops and displays:

```
?RW ERROR IN 2Ø
```

This error can be avoided by moving it past line 2Ø, and other problems avoided by adding an implied "GOTO" line 5Ø.

```
11Ø RESUME 5Ø
```

The Computer displays ?SN when a command, statement or function is misspelled or an operator is omitted. Type this **command**:

    RAN

Since the Computer cannot find the word RAN in its list of commands, it assumes you have misspelled something and displays the error message

    ?SN ERROR

SN (Syntax)
Code 2

This program demonstrates how the SN error can be generated by omitting an **operator**:

TEST PROGRAM

    1Ø REM 'SN' ERROR MESSAGE GENERATOR

    2Ø PRINT @474"HELLO OUT THERE"

RUN this program. The Computer is unable to find a comma in line 2Ø after the 474 so it halts and displays

    ?SN ERROR IN 2Ø

    READY

    2Ø_

The Computer automatically enters the EDIT mode when a SN error occurs **in a program**. The SN error generally occurs because of a typographical error.

To see the SN error caused by a misspelled **statement**, replace line 2Ø with

    2Ø PRIMT "I CAN'T SPELL PRINT"

This error message is displayed when string manipulation has become too complicated or too long for the Computer.

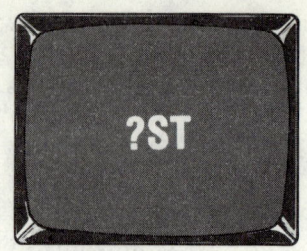

ST (String Formula Too Complex)
Code 16

To avoid typing a lengthly program in the Computer to demonstrate this error message, it can be simulated by typing in the following short program;

```
1Ø REM 'ST' ERROR MESSAGE PROGRAM

2Ø ERROR 16
```

RUN this program. The Computer displays the error message:

```
?ST ERROR IN 2Ø
```

Note: This error code is practically impossible to initiate in the BASIC used in the TRS-80 Level II.

?TM is displayed when a numeric value is assigned to a string variable or a string is assigned to a numeric variable.

**TM (Type Mismatch)
Code 13**

TEST PROGRAM

```
1Ø REM 'TM' ERROR MESSAGE GENERATOR

2Ø INPUT "ENTER ANY NUMBER";N

3Ø N$=N
```

SAMPLE RUN

```
ENTER ANY NUMBER? 5
?TM ERROR IN 3Ø
```

When a number is entered in line 2Ø, the Computer tries to assign this value to string variable N$ in line 3Ø. Since the two variables are not compatible, the program crashes.

RUN the program again and enter a letter instead of a number. The Computer gives you another chance to enter numeric data by displaying the error message

```
?REDO
```

and returns execution to the line where the error occurred.

Type Mismatching can be a real headache since strings tend to be confusing at times. Try RUNning each of these in the Test Program:

```
3Ø X=N$

3Ø IF N$=N GOTO 2Ø

3Ø X="R"*8

3Ø ON N$ GOTO 1Ø
```

Does this mean it's an X-rated program? Well, it may be X-ceptional if you ever actually see this error in the normal course of everyday programming.

?UE is displayed when the ERROR statement is used to self-inflict an error and the resulting error code is not one of the 23 used by the computer.

UE (Unprintable Error) Code 2Ø

For example, type the Command:

        ERROR 5Ø

The Computer checks its list of error codes and can't find this one. It lets you know about it by displaying the message:

        ?UE ERROR

TEST PROGRAM

        1Ø REM 'UE' ERROR MESSAGE PROGRAM

        2Ø ERROR 5Ø

SAMPEL RUN

        ?UE ERROR IN 2Ø

The same error message plus the line number containing the ERROR statement is printed when the error occurs inside a program.

Hmmmm. Very strange!

?UL is displayed when a branching statement such as GOTO or GOSUB calls for a line number that does not exist.

UL (Undefined Line)
Code 8

TEST PROGRAM

```
1Ø REM 'UL' ERROR MESSAGE GENERATOR
2Ø PRINT "I WILL NOW ATTEMPT TO GOTO LINE 5Ø"
3Ø GOTO 5Ø
4Ø REM THERE IS NO LINE 5Ø IN THIS PROGRAM
```

SAMPLE RUN

```
I WILL NOW ATTEMPT TO GOTO LINE 5Ø
?UL ERROR IN LINE 3Ø
```

The Computer displays the PRINT statement in line 2Ø, then attempts to GOTO line 5Ø. There being no line 5Ø, it stops and displays UL.

A UL error also occurs when GOTO and GOSUB statements are followed by a variable (not a number). Add these lines to the sample program:

```
25 N=2Ø
3Ø GOTO N
```

and RUN.

Although this is really more of a syntax error, the TRS-80 gives us a UL.

Finally, the UL error message is also displayed when the EDIT command calls for a line number not in use.

Type:

```
EDIT 1ØØ
```

The Computer responds with:

```
?UL ERROR
```

Appendix B: ASCII Code Table

Decimal Code	ASCII Character	Decimal Code	ASCII Character	Decimal Code	ASCII Character
32	space	63	?	94	→
33	!	64	@	95	–
34	"	65	A	97	a
35	#	66	B	98	b
36	$	67	C	99	c
37	%	68	D	100	d
38	&	69	E	101	e
39	'	70	F	102	f
40	(	71	G	103	g
41	)	72	H	104	h
42	*	73	I	105	i
43	+	74	J	106	j
44	,	75	K	107	k
45	–	76	L	108	l
46	.	77	M	109	m
47	/	78	N	110	n
48	0	79	O	111	o
49	1	80	P	112	p
50	2	81	Q	113	q
51	3	82	R	114	r
52	4	83	S	115	s
53	5	84	T	116	t
54	6	85	U	117	u
55	7	86	V	118	v
56	8	87	W	119	w
57	9	88	X	120	x
58	:	89	Y	121	y
59	;	90	Z	122	z
60	<	91	↑ or [	123	{
61	=	92	↓	124	\
62	>	93	←	125	}
				126	~

Summary of LEVEL 1 BASIC

(supplied for reference only)

Commands	Purpose	Example
NEW	Clears out all program lines stored in memory	NEW (not part of program)
RUN	Starts program execution at lowest-numbered line	RUN (not part of program)
RUN###	Starts program execution at specified line number	RUN 300 (not part of program)
LIST	Displays the first 12 program lines stored in memory, starting at lowest numbered line. Use ↟ key to display higher-numbered lines (if any)	LIST (not part of program)
LIST###	Same as LIST, but starts at specified line number	LIST 300 (not part of program)
CONT	Continues program execution when BREAK AT ### is displayed	CONT (not part of program)

Statements	Purpose	Example
PRINT	Prints value of a variable or expression; also prints whatever is inside quotes	10 PRINT "A+B="; A+B
INPUT	Tells Computer to let you enter data from the Keyboard	10 INPUT A,B,C
INPUT	Also has built-in PRINT capability	10 INPUT "ENTER A"; A
READ	Reads data in DATA statement	10 READ A,B,C,A$
DATA	Holds data to be read by READ statement	20 DATA 1,2,3, "SALLY"
RESTORE	Causes next READ statement to start with first item in first DATA line	30 RESTORE
LET	(Optional) Assigns a new value to variable on left of equals sign	0 LET A=3.14159
GOTO	Transfers program control to designated program line	10 GOTO 300

Statements	Purpose	Example
IF-THEN	Establishes a test point	1∅IF A=B THEN 3∅∅
FOR-NEXT	Sets up a do-loop to be executed a specified number of times	1∅ FOR I=1 TO 1∅ 2∅ NEXT I
STEP	Specifies size of increment to be used in FOR-NEXT loops	1∅ FOR I=∅ TO 1∅ STEP 2
STOP	Stops program execution and prints BREAK AT # # # message	1∅ IF A⟨B STOP
END	Ends program execution and sets program counter to zero	99 END
GOSUB	Transfers program control to subroutine beginning at specified line	1∅ GOSUB 3∅∅∅
RETURN	Ends subroutine execution and returns control to GOSUB line	3∅1∅ RETURN
ON	Multi-way branch used with GOTO and GOSUB.	1∅ ON N GOTO 3∅,4∅,5∅ 1∅ ON N GOSUB 3∅∅∅, 4∅∅∅, 5∅∅∅

Print Modifiers	Purpose	Example
AT	(Follows PRINT) Begins printing at specified location on Display	1∅ PRINT AT 65∅, "HELLO"
TAB	(Follows PRINT) Begins printing at specified number of spaces from left margin	1∅ PRINT TAB (1∅); "MONTH"; TAB (2∅); "RECEIPTS"

Graphic Statements	Purpose	Example
SET	Lights up a specified location on Display	1∅ SET (3∅,4∅)
RESET	Turns off a specified graphics location on Display	2∅ RESET (3∅,4∅)
POINT	Checks the specified graphics location: if point is "on", returns a 1; if "off", returns a ∅.	3∅ IF POINT (3∅,4∅)=1 THEN PRINT "ON"
CLS	Turns off all graphics locations (clears screen)	1∅ CLS

Built-In Functions	Description	Example
MEM	Returns the number of free bytes left in memory	1Ø PRINT MEM
INT(X)	Returns the greatest integer which is less than or equal to X (-32768< x< 32768)	1Ø I=INT (Y)
ABS(X)	Absolute value of X	1Ø M=ABS (A)
RND (Ø)	Returns a random number between Ø and 1	1Ø X=RND(Ø)
RND(N)	Returns a random integer between 1 and N (1≤ N< 32768)	1Ø X=RND(5ØØ)

Math Operators	Function	Example
+	Addition	A+B
−	Subtraction	A−B
*	Multiplication	A*B
/	Division	A/B
=	Assigns value of right-hand side to variable on left-hand side	A=B

Relational Operators	Relationship	Example
<	Is less than	A<B
>	Is greater than	A>B
=	Is equal to	A=B
<=	Is less than or equal to	A<=B
>=	Is greater than or equal to	A>=B
<>	Is not equal to	A<>B

Logical Operators	Function	Example
*	AND	(A=3)*(B=7) "A equals 3 and B equals 7"
+	OR	(A=3)+(B=7) "A equals 3 or B equals 7"

Summary of LEVEL I BASIC—continued

Variables	Purpose	Example
A through Z	Take on number values	A=3.14159
A$ and B$	Take on string values (up to 16 characters)	A$=RADIO SHACK
A(X)	Store the elements of a one-dimensional array (X≤MEM/4-1)	A(∅)=4∅∅

LEVEL I Shorthand Dialect

Command/Statement	Abbreviation	Command/Statement	Abbreviation
PRINT	P.	TAB (after PRINT)	T.
NEW	N.	INT	I.
RUN	R.	GOSUB	GOS.
LIST	L.	RETURN	RET.
END	E.	READ	REA.
THEN	T.	DATA	D.
GOTO	G.	RESTORE	REST.
INPUT	IN.	ABS	A.
MEM	M.	RND	R.
FOR	F.	SET	S.
NEXT	N.	RESET	R.
STEP (after FOR)	S.	POINT	P.
STOP	ST.	PRINT AT	P.A.
CONT	C.	CLOAD	CL.
CLS?	C	CSAVE	CS.
INPUT			IN or I

Level II Reserved Words*

@	FN	PEEK
ABS	FOR	POINT
AND	FORMAT	POKE
APPEND	FRE	POS
ASC	FREE	POSN
ATN	GET	PRINT
AUTO	GOSUB	PUT
CDBL	GOTO	RANDOM
CHR$	IF	READ
CINT	INKEY$	REM
CLEAR	INP	RENAME
CLOCK	INPUT	RESET
CLOSE	INSTR	RESTORE
CLS	INT	RESUME
CMD	KILL	RETURN
CONT	LEFT$	RIGHT$
COS	LET	RND
CSNG	LSET	RSET
CVD	LEN	SAVE
CVI	LINE	SET
CVS	LIST	SGN
DATA	LOAD	SIN
DEFDBL	LOC	SQR
DEFFN	LOF	STEP
DEFINT	LOG	STOP
DEFSNG	MEM	STRING$
DEFUSR	MERGE	STR$
DEFSTR	MID$	TAB
DELETE	MKD$	TAN
DIM	MKI$	THEN
EDIT	MKS$	TIME$
ELSE	NAME	TO
END	NEW	TROFF
EOF	NEXT	TRON
ERL	NOT	USING
ERR	ON	USR
ERROR	OPEN	VAL
EXP	OR	VARPTR
FIELD	OUT	VERIFY
FIX		

*Many of these words have no function in LEVEL II BASIC; they are reserved for use in LEVEL II BASIC DISK. None of these words can be used inside a variable name. You'll get a syntax error if you try to use these words as variables.

Appendix Z: Cut and Paste Section for

LEVEL I Manual

Index for Parts II and III of *Learning Level II*

For Additional Copies

of

Learning Level II

Contact your local Computer, Electronics or Book Store

or

Send $15.95 each + $1.45 Postage & Handling to

COMPUSOFT PUBLISHING
P. O. Box 19669-P
San Diego, CA 92119
(California addresses add 6% sales tax)

Educational Discounts available for quantity purchases.

Write for details.

ISBN #0-932760-01-5